TABBOO!

TABBOO!
1982–88

GORDON ROBICHAUX
KARMA

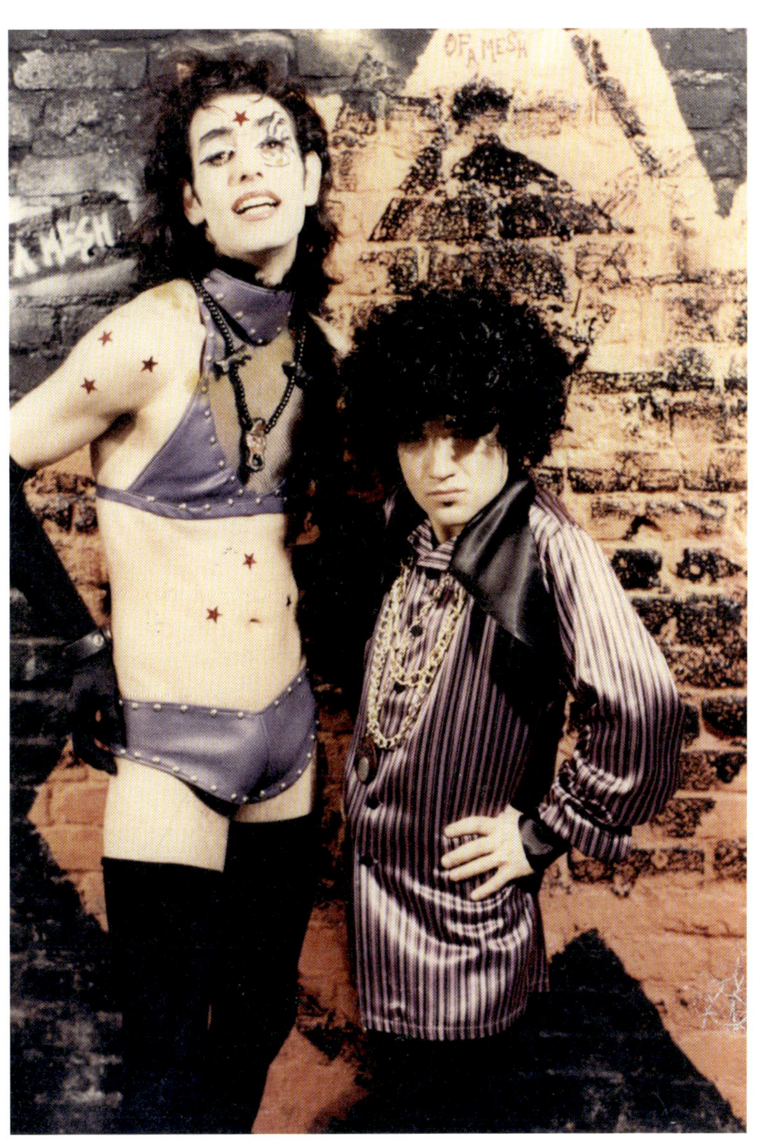
OF A MESH
A MESH

VOICE THROUGH A SPIRAL

JARRETT EARNEST

!

The artist Tabboo!, henceforth referred to as Glamorous Life, declares in looping monologue through the whirlwind of time: "*Oh*, I'm known for my *flowers*!"

!

A ruffled peony might be deemed *beautiful* in a garden, even excruciatingly so, but could never be *glamorous*. Those same blooms, however—cut, arranged, and slipped into a vase, or tucked behind an ear—can epitomize glamour itself. The distinction is one of intention, intervention, and degree of artifice.

!

Glamorous Life interjects: "*Art Nouveau.* Deco is great but Art Nouveau comes out on top because Art Nouveau is *nat-u-ral* ... I love *flowers* and *plants*—I grew up in the country—I love nature, and there isn't a straight line in nature really, it's all *curves* and it's all so *inspirational*—ooohh! The ocean! Stars! Trees! Wind!—*I love it all!* Even when I do cityscapes there's not a straight line in there—I would be fired, they would take my blueprints and rip 'em up!—I'm like a *curly-do witch*."

!

Glamour is calculated, anticipating perception. It leans toward a tipping point of absurdity and exaggeration, rubbing against the grain of received expectation, flirting with embarrassment or shame or awkwardness only to add suspense, and emphasize its success.

!

In his lyrical treatise on the subject of "The Glamorous Life," Prince, the purple-paisley expert, captures it all casually in the opening line: "She wears a long fur coat of mink / Even in the summertime."

!

Consider a bouquet of cheap flowers tucked into an empty red-and-yellow El Pico coffee can, both picked up from the bodega on the corner to form a still life to be painted by Glamorous Life in her Alphabet City apartment. The gaily nondescript flowers hover above a whirl of stems: clouds of neon pink, electric robin's egg blue, tangerine tapering into pastel blushes, all set against a field of lush yellows, goldenrod to canary to butter, imbedded with a spray of actual gold glitter. Along the left side a glittering blue swath, pulled aside, like a repoussoir curtain, as though unveiling the scene to an audience—*tah-dah!*—a magic show revelation. At 52 by 38 inches it's much larger than life, granting grandeur. Vivid colors and glittering surfaces provide the razzle dazzle and command attention like a cabaret act. The painting is titled *You Can Only Get It in New York*—"That's showbiz!"

!

The art of Glamorous Life—paintings, sets, costumes, performances, ephemera—is a degree-zero case study of the operations of glamour in its most elemental state.

!

Glamorous Life recalls early formation in the Massachusetts countryside in the 1960s: "I grew up in a working-class family where there wasn't much glamour. I had an aunt who once came to a funeral in an ostrich boa and I was like, 'What is that?!' Once in a while my mother would go to church in a crow feather hat, spiky heels and a red lip, but for the most part, she was a simple country girl. It was *Little House on the Prairie*-type shit, so glamour was from TV or movies, and one of the biggest movies that still affects me to this day like nothing else was *The Wizard of Oz*—Judy Garland, Glinda the Good Witch, and even the Wicked Witch of the West were so fucking glamorous, and all done by that Jewish gay guy from Brooklyn named 'Adrian'—without the costumes, have you seen what those people look like in real life? Actually Billie Burke, the wife of Florenz Ziegfeld, was always glamorous, but Judy—*not so much!* She's gorgeous in that movie. And that's thanks to another gay guy, George Cukor. He was on that movie for five minutes and looked at Judy and said, 'Why does she look like that? Give me that thing, take that off!' The Dorothy we know was because of George Cukor ..."

!

Consider also the stem of a top-heavy tulip, as it bends imperceptibly deeper by the hour from the lip of a vase—understated glamour.

!

In classical geometry a curve is defined as the most glamorous path from point A to point B. That's a mathematical fact.

For proof, see Mae West on cadence: "I liked long words. There was a rhythm in their many syllables, and I would pronounce them slowly to savor their swing. That's why I was later able to make such words as *fas-cin-atin'* acquire an individual connotation. I also liked to reverse natural word order to get a better rhythm into my speech."

!

Glamorous Life visits contemporary art shows and is displeased: "I have no hatred of it, I'm just saying, a lot of this stuff in 'real' art galleries—every time I walk into those places I just want to throw tomatoes. It doesn't even make me angry, I'm just *bored*, which is the biggest insult."

!

Originally the English word *glamour* was a verb, meaning to deceive or charm by means of an illusion, most likely conjured by magic. A curve ball. A curly-q.

!

Glamorous Life, once dubbed the "Daffy Duck of Drag," narrates infelicities of changing contexts: "I had a friend who thought glamour was negative, was cheap and fake—if it's glamour, then it's not 'real art.' All through that time I had a big bone of—*contentment?*—whatever that saying is—that they wouldn't let me into the art world because I did drag! As you might know, I was very popular—*some* say more popular than RuPaul. She was *prettier*, well, depending—*whatever.* I thought they didn't like me because glamour and art didn't go together.

"My friend Pat Hearn, she was very glamorous. You can be glamorous and be the dealer because that makes the limos roll up. Like Patti Astor or Mary Boone. That's why Andy Warhol surrounded himself with drag queens and movie stars and Halston because, left to himself, he's just a bald-headed speckled twerp, you know what I mean? But the glamour of it all with Edie Sedgwick and Joe D'Alessandro—I want some of that!—otherwise it's just a Campbell's soup can, and who doesn't have one of those?"

!

An undulant crimson background embedded with layers of glitter, overpainted, leaving granular textures amid exposed twinkle. The bottom is a pink shelf, a shallow proscenium, presenting three objects on stage. From left to right: a pale ceramic poodle standing at attention with a pink bow around its neck; a cream-colored vase shaped like a woman's head, her shoulder-length hair flipping out the sides with a fuchsia crumple of flowers peeking out the top of her scalp; a tall, slender "Oriental" doll, wrapped in pearlescent fabric, with a translucent veil across the bottom of her face. As inanimate objects, they are still and waiting, ever ready to be enjoyed by being looked at; ideal subject matter for a painting by Glamorous Life, titled *The Beautiful Ones*.

!

Glamorous Life evokes sensuous material memories: "Back in the early sixties, one of the major forms of entertainment was puppetry, especially for children—and I was a professional puppeteer as a child. I'd make my own puppets. 'What do you want for Christmas?'—I'd want fabrics. My most favorite fabric was velvet—if I *ever* got a hold of a piece of velvet I was giddy—he-he-he! I had this little doll that had a dark cranberry velvet jacket—I just couldn't believe, I'd never seen anyone in real life wear something like that ..."

!

A tabletop cityscape of red, yellow, and blue tin cans enlarged to epic proportions on their 78-by-48-inch canvas. The stacked-can architecture—mostly tomatoes, one labeled *Guido*—are populated by puppet and doll heads: Hanna-Barbera's Ricochet Rabbit grins, buck-toothed; a plastic Tweety head lies nearby, looking up; a large plastic Lambchop head, saved from childhood—Glamorous Life's oldest personal possession. To the right a Kewpie sticks out of a big yellow can labeled "pasta," surveying the scene with unshakable affection like a cheerful Oscar the Grouch. The space behind them is buzzing cobalt with perfectly calibrated torrents of blue glitter. Presiding at the top of the canvas is a rectangular image of an eye with thick lashes, like a sun or moon looking down—it is the eye of Tabboo!, the Pyramid Club's own Eye of Horus. From the top right edge, the outline of a purple iris and single leaf peeks in, giving a vaudeville wave at the curtain's edge. The painting is fast, drips running down to negative space at the bottom, with just enough brushwork to convey the effect, to give it life. It is the essence of performance—the characters are ready to put on a show, to hold your attention, to garner your adulation. This array is not junk at all, it's a play.

!

Glamorous Life self-analyzes: "With performing—and I've been performing since I was a child—you'd make posters to advertise your shows. Instead of writing formally I was always flourishing my lines. But in the '80s everything was very hard-edge and block letters and since I was doing my own posters—if everyone is doing one thing *I'll do the other*, purposely, so I can be *seen*, because I like to be seen and I'm loud and I want to be seen. There is only one star in a Helen Lawson production and that's *me—Tabboo!*"

!

The particular truth Glamorous Life demonstrates is that the poorest materials, the cheapest effects, can be orchestrated to rival even the most rarefied riches. This was the great revelation of Jack Smith, New York's Old Testament prophet of glamour. Indeed, this bodega alchemy is actually glamour of a higher order because the transformation travels a farther distance, rendering its gesture more profound. A diamond is a highly constructed cultural object, diagrammed for maximum sparkle and conferred status by means of material scarcity. If that visual effect can be rivaled by Swarovski crystal, all the better—you can use even more. But when those replica crystals are translated into rhinestones, and then even more roughly iterated as sequins and glitter—flecks of ground plastic garbage in its crudest form—the semiotic chain is actually moving upward, toward the heights of glamour. To pull off glitter as precious jewels requires ever greater powers of self-confidence, artifice, desire, and belief. A diamond doesn't need your validation for its own worth—its unique properties are well defended by a massive edifice of capital; but this glamour born of trash lives and dies by our intention and attention, exactly the way Tinkerbell does. Exacting a price which imagination repays in full.

!

Glamorous Life advises (referring to this very text): "Drop the word *chic* in there somewhere—in a positive way."

!

Glamorous Life recounts personal artistic philosophy: "My generation was the first generation that came of age post-Stonewall—*we're here, were queer, get used to it!* I don't do gay art shit, like showing cock and balls with a hairy ass—mine is gay like *The Women*, like a Technicolor movie with Adrian costumes ... Gay as a *glamorous* thing—what's the word? *Aesthetic!* You know what I mean?"

!

At some point Glamorous Life looked at the alphabet and thought—*not enough curves*. Like a queen overdrawing her lips or padding a bra, Glamorous Life remade the letters of the alphabet, inviting them to giggle, shimmer, and bounce, recasting each of the twenty-six letters in her own image, titled *Self-Portrait in Drag*.

!

As chief maker of posters, T-shirts, and backdrops for the Pyramid Club on Avenue A, Glamorous Life made over the look of Alphabet City during the neighborhood's heyday as countercultural cross-pollinator. Her distinctive, swooning hand lettering moved far beyond the confines of Lower Manhattan when Glamorous Life drew the logo and did the graphic design for the debut release of crossover dance sensation Deee-Lite, fronted by glamour's archangel Lady Miss Kier, propelled around the world by their hit single "Groove Is in the Heart."

!

Glamorous Life accounts for the tricky business of influence within a scene: "I do everything handmade—I'm a *handmade queen*! My posters are like that. All my letters and all my ads for the Pyramid—it was the mecca of the downtown art world, and I was the *look*! So it got everywhere. Then *Paper* magazine came around and they started hiring me to do a page for every single issue, then they wanted all their advertisers to make it look like *me*. Then Prince started copying me and David Bowie started copying me. Janet Jackson copied me. Madonna ..."

!

“She saw him standing in the section marked / ‘If you have to ask, you can’t afford it’ lingerie (lingerie)” —Prince, “The Glamorous Life”

!

As a force glamour is coded feminine, which doesn’t mean female in a biological sense. Our greatest theoreticians of glamour—Mae West, Eartha Kitt, Cookie Mueller—are often deemed “female drag queens” in ham-fisted attempts to explain how far their aesthetic performance outpaces cultural norms. They resemble the category of “woman” as much as an Art Nouveau railing resembles a rosebush, which is to say, not at all, except as the most fabulous dream. And it is precisely by means of this baroque artifice that their genius radiates.

!

“He’s not vicious or malicious / Just de-lovely and delicious”—Deee-Lite, “Groove Is in the Heart”

!

In *Wigstock*, the eponymously named documentary about the legendary drag festival, Glamorous Life performs on an outdoor stage in Tompkins Square Park wearing a sixties minidress made from a peach silk sari, the hem riding up right above the bedazzled bulge of her thong. Her face is framed by a dark wig with distinctive bangs à la Liza as Sally Bowles, while eight-inch punk spikes stick up around the back, matching her studded collar. In an exaggeratedly accented rap to funky arhythmic backing tracks, Glamorous Life repeats “it’s na-tu-ral” in a grating nasal shriek: “Draaag! Are they girls or boys? Draaag! Are they girls or boys? Draaag! Bok-bok-bok! I can’t figure it out! It’s natural! ... girls, it’s natural! For me—it’s natural! It’s natural!”

!

"There was a point where every single person I knew was what is now called *non-binary*—a drag queen or she-male or whatever. *Everyone*. I didn't know gay men! Recently somebody asked me if I was in ACT UP—oh no honey, that was for butch queens with good bodies and cute faces—that wasn't for drag queens. There was a huge throwdown at Wigstock one year when there was a fag-bashing and they said, 'Stop Wigstock, we have to take it over for ...' The queens yelled back, 'Get the fuck off the stage!'"

!

"I don't like a big commotion, I'm a demon for slow motion or such / Why should I deny that I would die to know a guy what takes his time" —Mae West, "A Guy What Takes His Time"

!

Glamorous Life waxes poetic on the import of sparkle: "The glitter makes it come *alive.* Like when Judy walks into—it's the Technicolor! *Wooo! Glitter in the air! The faerie dust!* Like when you see a Jack Smith movie, or the sequins on a Marlene Dietrich gown ... they're glittery, and at the same time they're just an El Pico coffee can, so *down-home*, rich and poor—*boom-boom*!"

!

"Paint a perfect picture / Bring 2 life a vision in one's mind / The beautiful ones / Always smash the picture / Always every time" —Prince, "The Beautiful Ones"

!

The head and shoulders are turned three-quarters like a demented *Mona Lisa*—face and neck a deep green patina of an Ancient Greek bronze, complete with incised, vacant, almond-shaped eyes. Rows of glistening mauve teeth are offset by fluorescent coral lips. A swooping blue-and-aqua hairdo pushes beyond the top of the canvas, cascading down to rest in front of the shoulder. The figure is backlit by a searing salmon-and-yellow background: a diagonal Greek column with a fancy Corinthian capital tumbles behind her. Scratched into the yellow ground are the words "Fall Fall Hairdo Hairdo Fall Fall"—a chant collapsing the fall of Rome with a fall, a hairpiece designed to blend in with natural hair. The subject is Glamorous Life herself, painted as a twenty-five-year-old in drag, a classical beauty, a goofball Helen of Troy.

!

There is a gravitas to glamour which needs no explanation beyond the pleasure it takes in being beheld, reciprocally *delighting* in inspiring *delight*. In this way its narcissism is transmuted into an invaluable social gift, with its power to organize haphazard audiences connected by their appreciation: all efflorescences of glamour are in some sense subcultural.

!

Glamorous Life explains the interior meaning of studio life: "It's where I meditate, where I commune with god, my higher power—I'm alone. I usually wake up at two, three in the morning, the paintings are done by 8:00 a.m. No one is around. The phone doesn't ring. Dawn is coming up. The plants and all the tchotchkes and my own little things ..."

!

Glamour appears in our lives in the way divinity becomes manifest in Renaissance paintings, with curved wings, whirlpooled robes, and serpentine ribbons—an event, as if out of nowhere, which one hardly deserves. Glamour heralds a belief that this could be *better*—more beautiful, exciting, voluptuous, or, in some important way, *different*—than it is. As an aesthetic attitude, glamour is itself closer to religion, a worldview.

!

"Sixty-one years of life experience and I've worked almost daily since on the *majesty* of the craft—is that the word? I'm really good now; I'm a master. In fact, recently, an extremely famous painter came into an exhibition and said, 'Ooh, I love this one! Who did this one?!'—That's a Tabboo! 'That's a Tabboo?!' he says. 'He's a master of his craft! He really knows how to paint! This is next-level shit!'—I'm paraphrasing—'How many more does he got?' He's got that one and that one and that one. He said, 'Wrap 'em up!'"

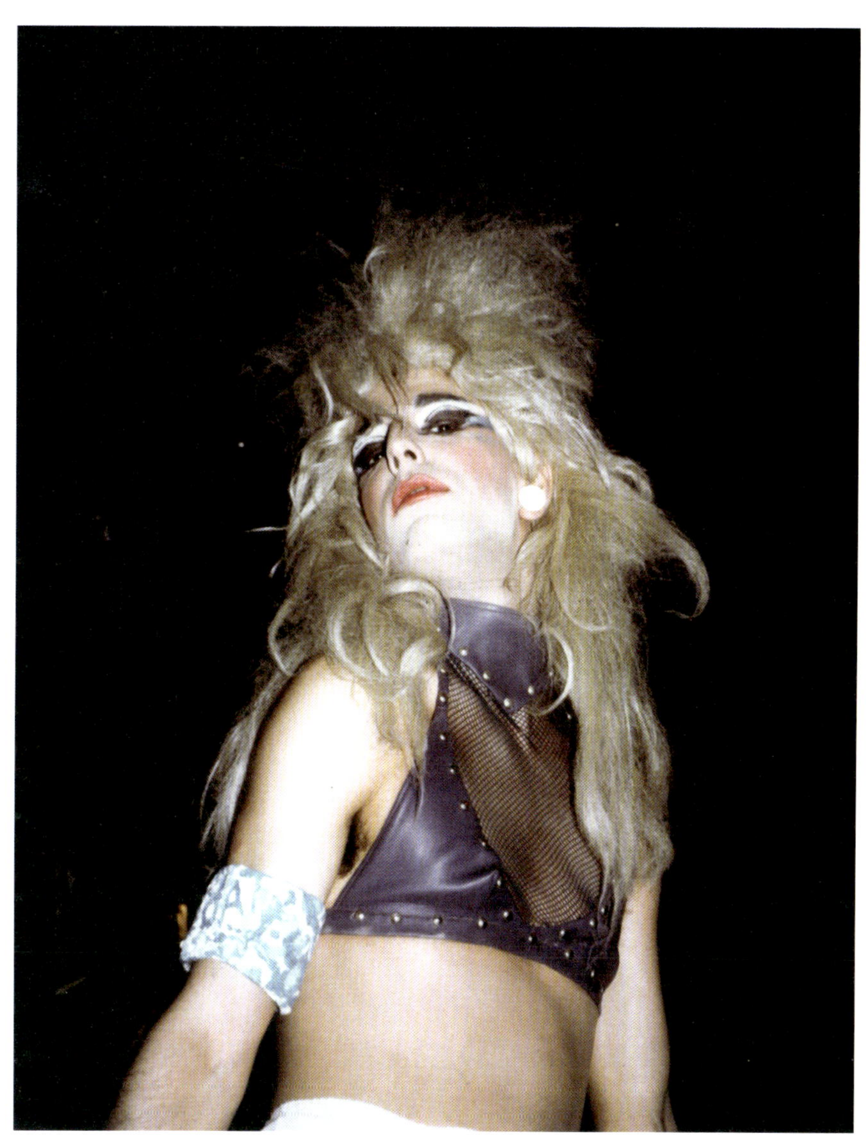

The first time I met Pat was probably around 1977—the year Elvis died—when we were both going to art school in Boston: I was at the Massachusetts College of Art and Design, *for poor people*, and she was at the Museum School. She had a shaved head and crazy eyebrows and makeup, and she wore wild psychedelic clothing. We hooked up immediately and started working together in Boston's performance art scene, which was really small. But we couldn't stay there forever. Pat got me to New York. She said, "Throw everything you've got in a garbage bag and let's move." She was a little more aggressive than I was, which sometimes can be good. But the very first day we got here, we were like, "Oh my God, did we make a mistake? What the fuck are we doing here?! We can't afford the rent!" So we thought, "Well, let's get out and just see the world, let's go to the Kitchen, let's go to White Columns." So one day we went to White Columns, and the show there was by somebody who took Barbie dolls, sculpted their hair, xeroxed them, and then put the copies all along the walls. There were people there performing, a boy and a girl, probably the same age. She was singing, and he was beating some drums and wearing a hula skirt. So we walked up to them and started talking. The woman was Ann Craig—a big star of downtown. The guy in the hula skirt was Jean-Michel Basquiat. I was like, "I think we're home."

Pat and I had a little No Wave band called Wild and Wonderful—it started in Boston. (It wasn't my first band, though—Jack Pierson, a bunch of other people, and I were in one called the Fucking Barbies.) We'd do things like slowly play Elvis's "That's When Your Heartaches Begin" backwards and sing over it. Pat would usually do the song, and I'd be playing drums. We were part of the scene that was based around Club 57 during the late 1970s and early '80s. We did shows everywhere: the Mudd Club, CBGB, Club 57, the Pyramid Club. That's how I met all those queens from Atlanta, like RuPaul and Lady Bunny. The Pyramid queens used to put on these theme nights at the clubs, too, like Old South Night, Trailer Park Trash Night, or Coney Island Baby Night.

Back then, I found my art supplies on the street. I'd scavenge through the trash of shipping and packing companies and find rolls of this disposable packing paper, like craft paper—something you'd wrap dead fish in. I once found all this Pepsodent toothpaste packaging and started painting on it. That stuff is not supposed to last, but I thought the world was going to end in 1984, or turn into something out of George Orwell, so I didn't care about doing things on 100 percent cotton rag acid-free paper. At the time, it was all about the Weimar Republic. That was the zeitgeist. It was coming out of punk, New Wave, and maybe the German stuff too: Kraftwerk, Klaus Nomi. I was inspired by German Expressionism, *Neue Sachlichkeit*, Otto Dix, all of that. One of my favorite movies is *Cabaret*—because of Bob Fosse, not just Liza Minnelli! I even met Nomi on my second day in New York. He tried to pick me up. He was a leather queen, alas. I wasn't into it. But it was such a big deal to meet him.

Tabboo!
as told to Alex Jovanovich

Originally published on
artforum.com, September 21, 2017

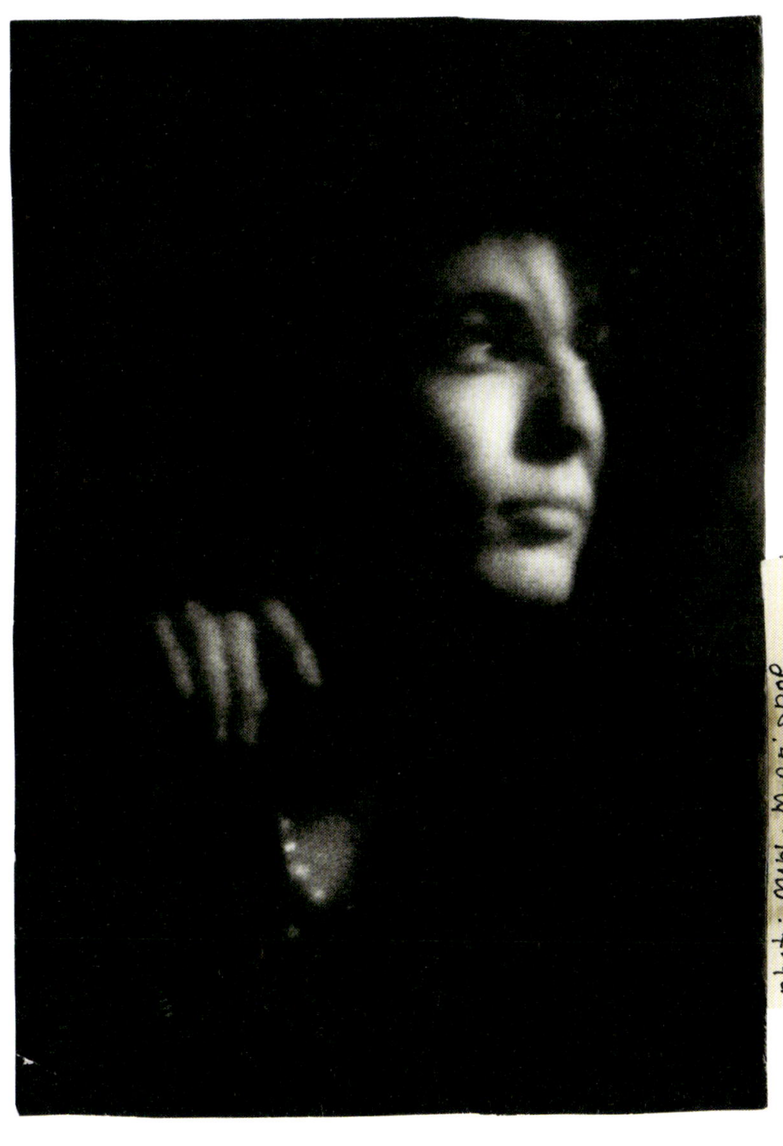
photo: MARK MORRISROE

Back in the day, downtown was mostly factories, and many were going out of business. I'd say this was around 1984: I was walking down 14th Street and this huge glitter factory had closed, and they'd dumped their deadstock onto the street. Boxes and boxes of old-school glitter. The kind that's illegal now. It cuts your eyes. You can't get this shit at Michaels. Every single color just like the paint chips at Sherwin-Williams: magenta, light blue, steel grays, light greens ... As soon as I opened one of the boxes and the sun hit the glitter, my head exploded, and other people started grabbing the boxes, like pigeons to crumbs. I grabbed as many as I could—maybe forty-five boxes—and ran home and back to get more. I knew right away I wanted to use the glitter in the paintings, just like when we threw glitter onto Jackie Curtis's coffin.

Tabboo!
as told to Jacob Robichaux

PLATES

Self-Portrait, 1982
Acrylic on found paper board
27 × 20¼ inches (68.6 × 51.4 cm)

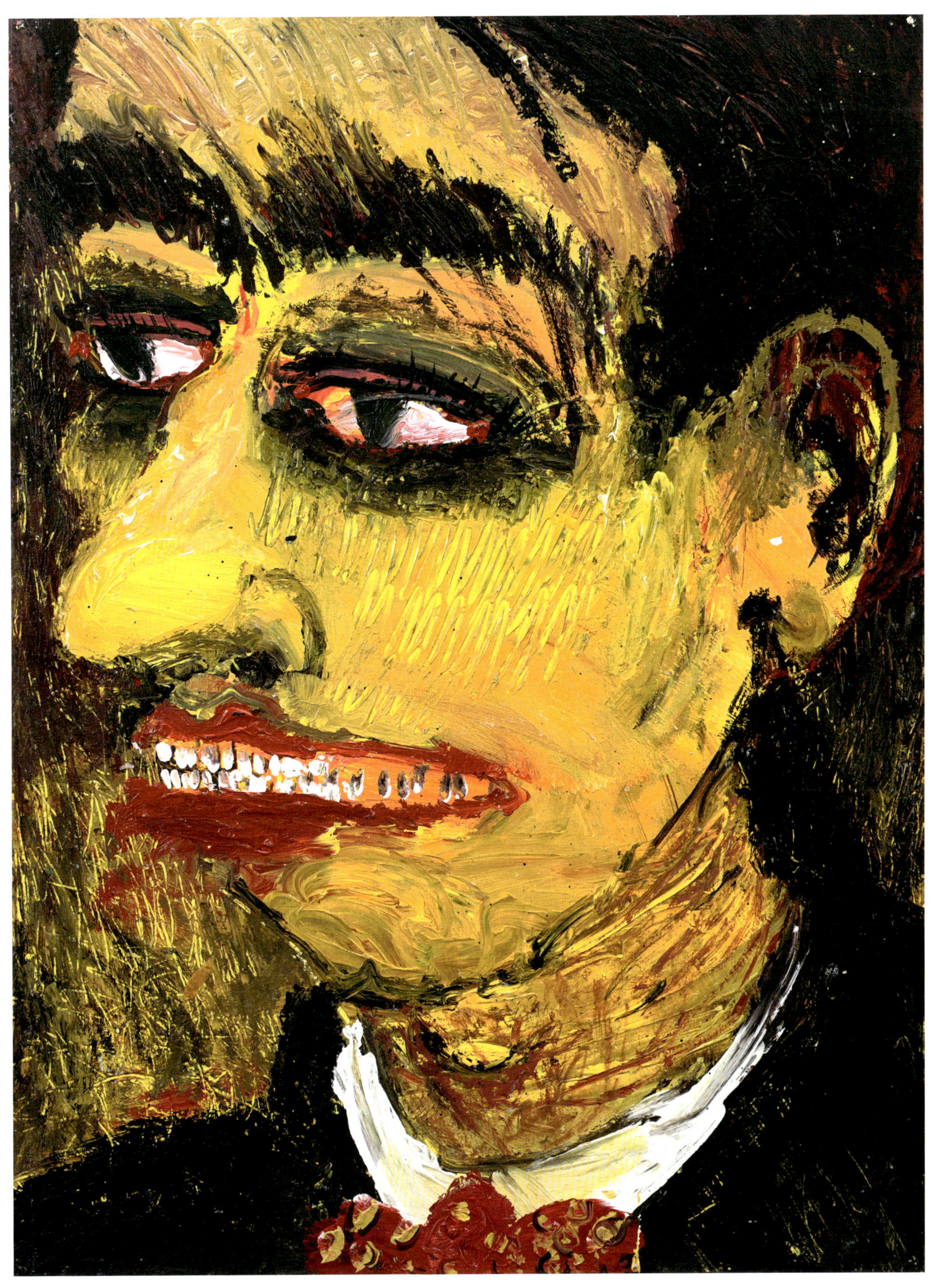

Self-Portrait in Drag, 1982
Acrylic on found paper board
27 × 20¼ inches (68.6 × 51.4 cm)

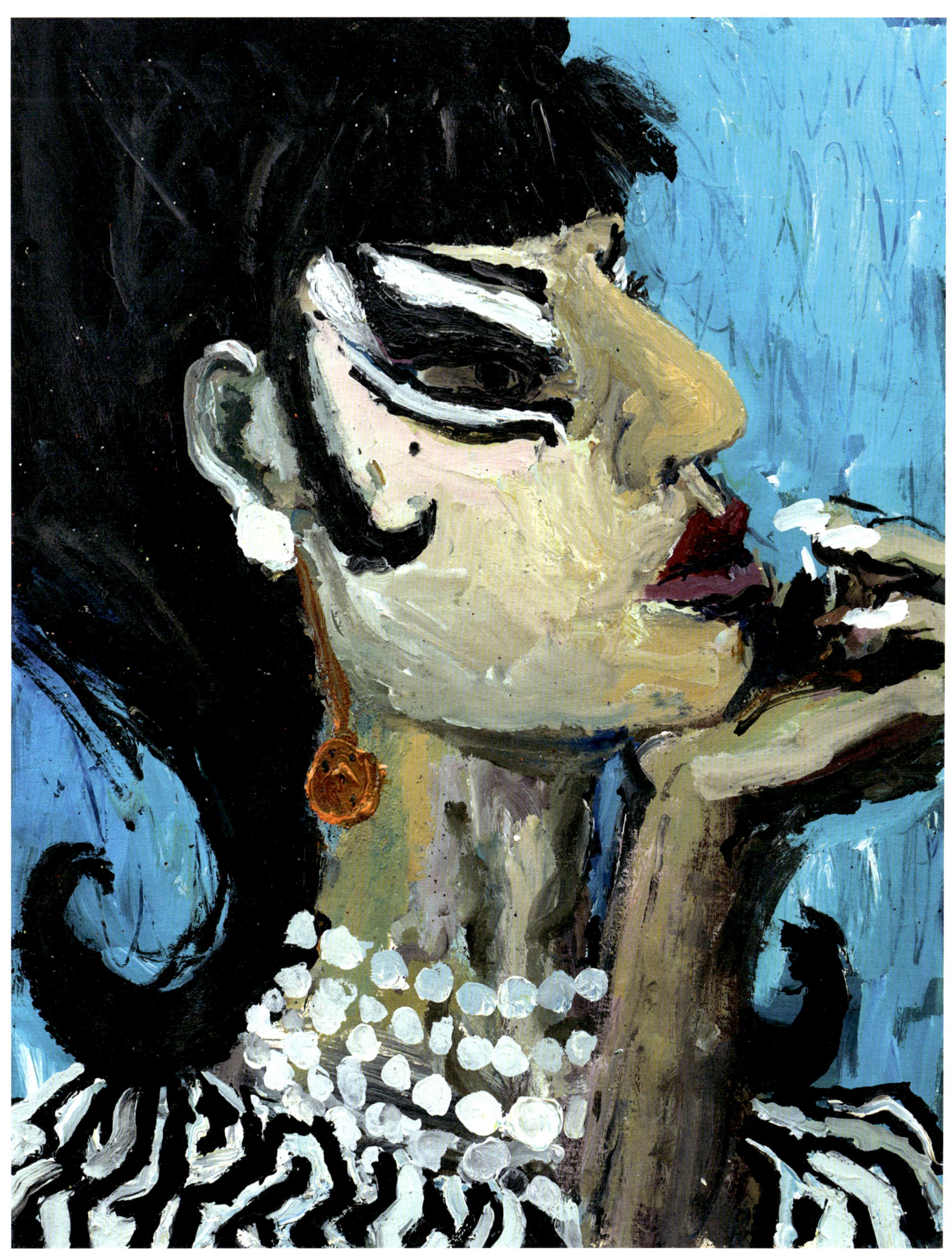

Self-Portrait in Drag as Popcorn, 1982
Acrylic on found paper board
27 × 20¼ inches (68.6 × 51.4 cm)

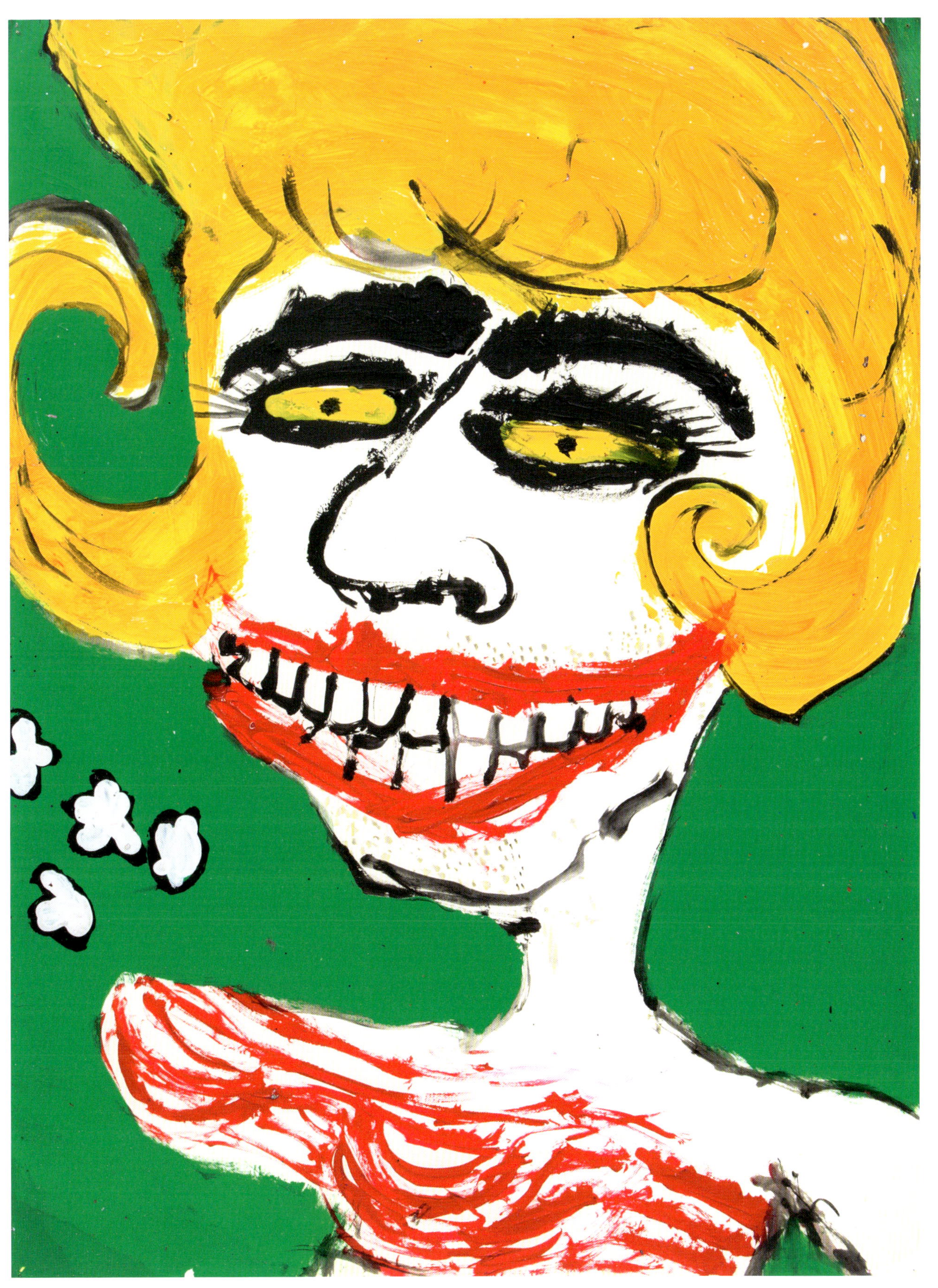

Connie Francis at San Janero Festival, 1982
Acrylic and glitter on found paper board
27 × 20 inches (68.6 × 50.8 cm)

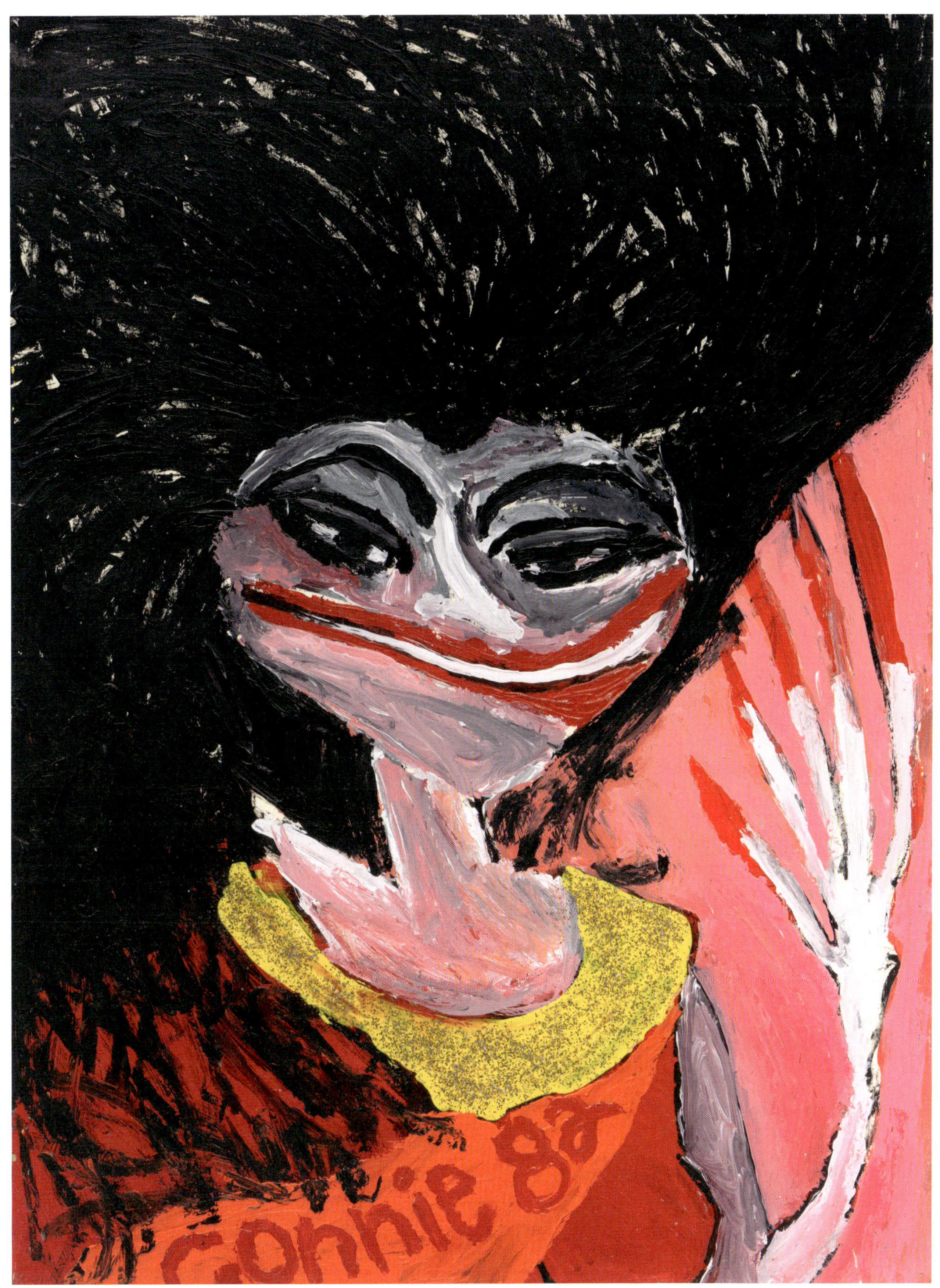
Connie 87

Self-Portrait, 1982
Acrylic on found paper board
27 × 20¼ inches (68.6 × 51.4 cm)

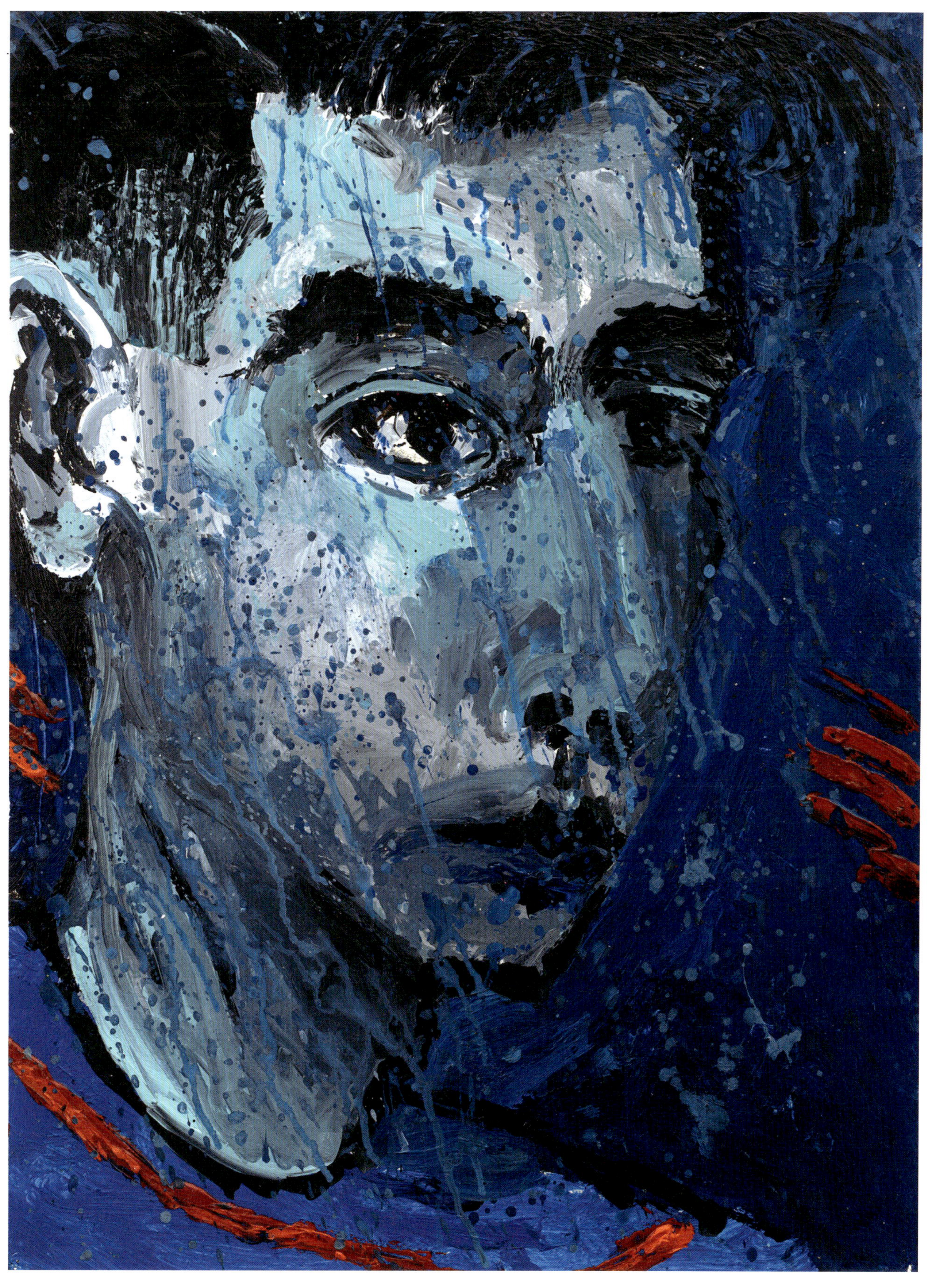

Untitled, 1982
Acrylic on found paper board
27 × 20¼ inches (68.6 × 51.4 cm)

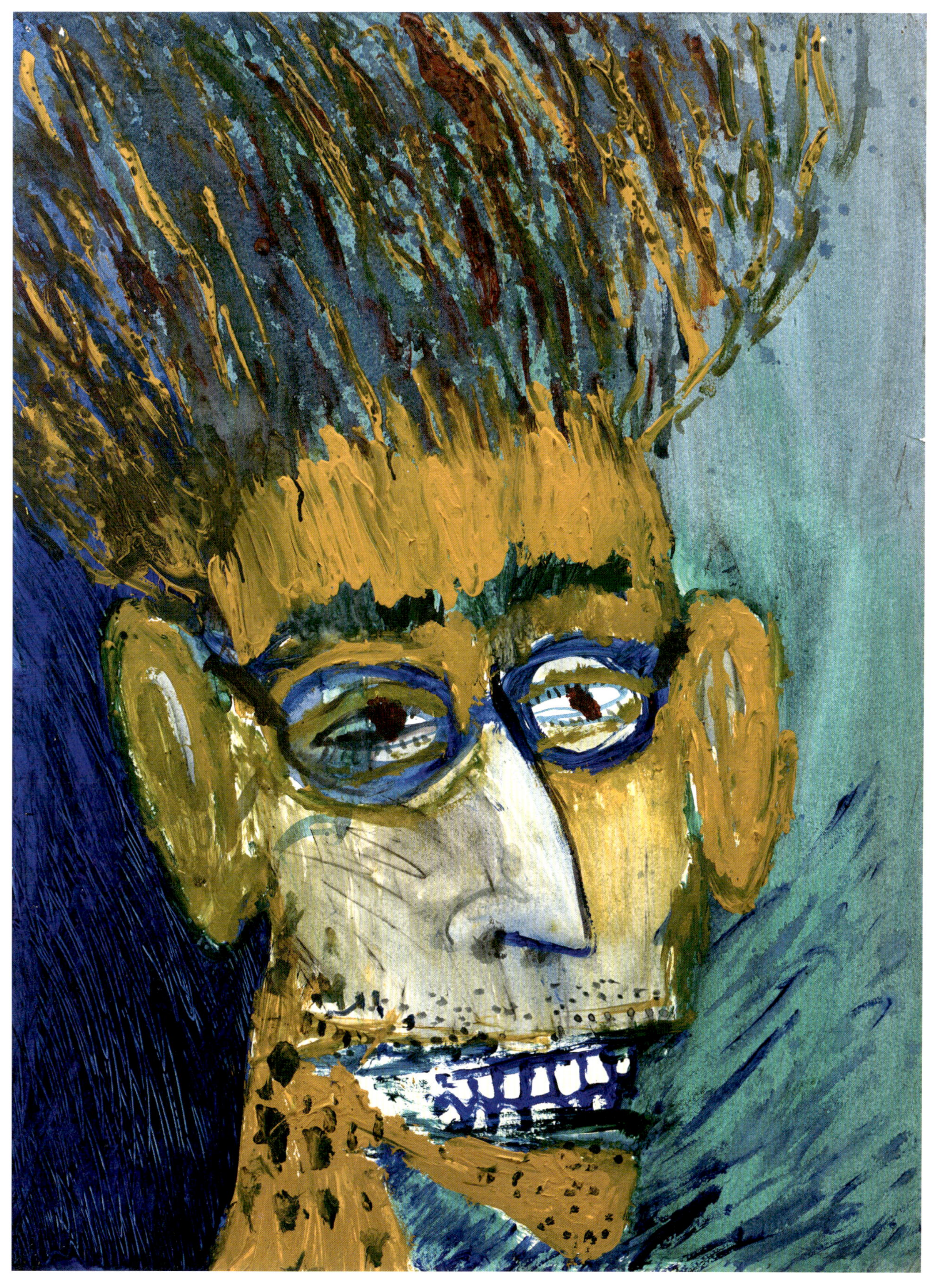

Spanish Lucy Drag, 1984
Acrylic on paper
24 × 20 inches (61 × 50.8 cm)

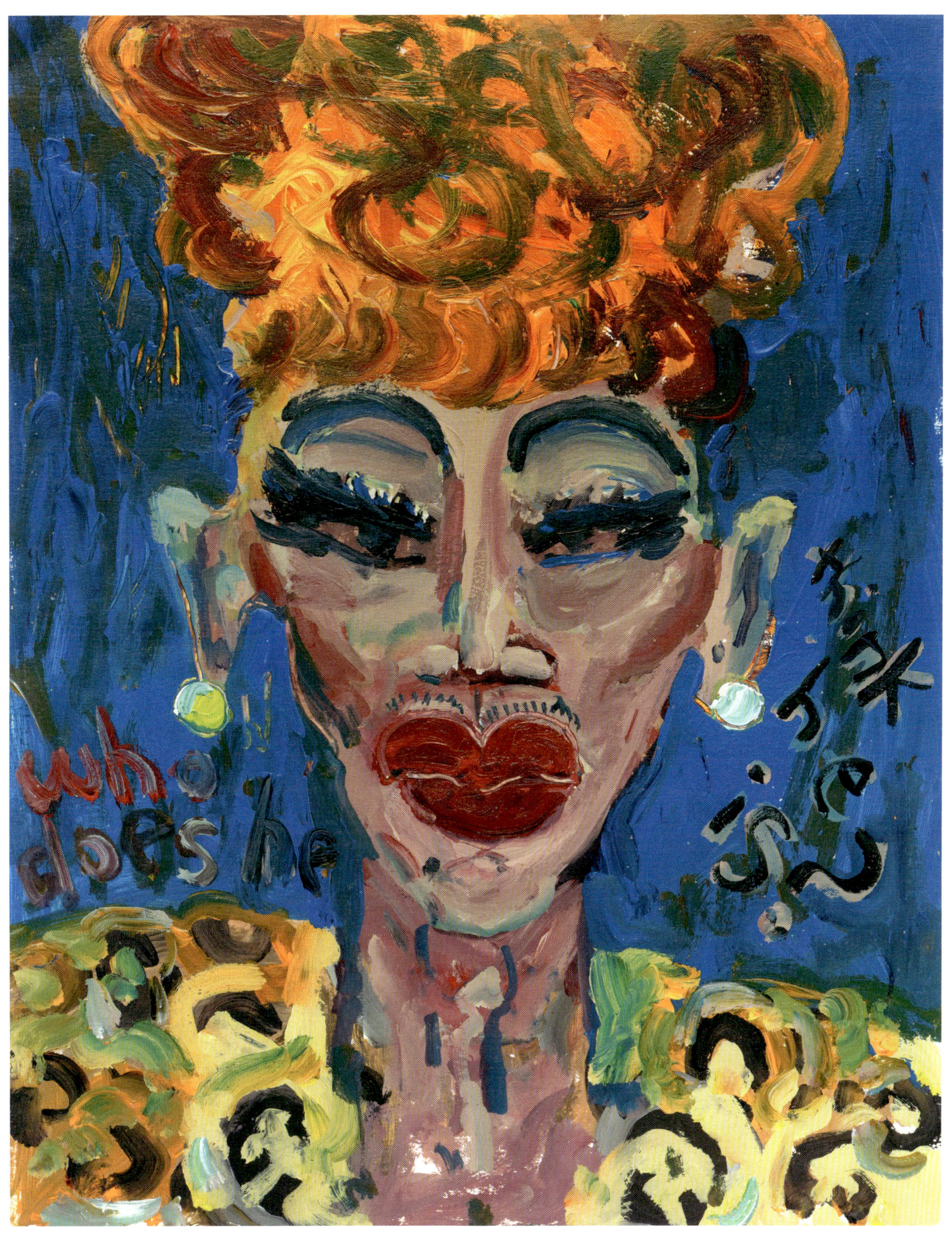
who
does he
think
he
is?

Lamb Chop, 1982
Acrylic on found paper board
27 × 20¼ inches (68.6 × 51.4 cm)

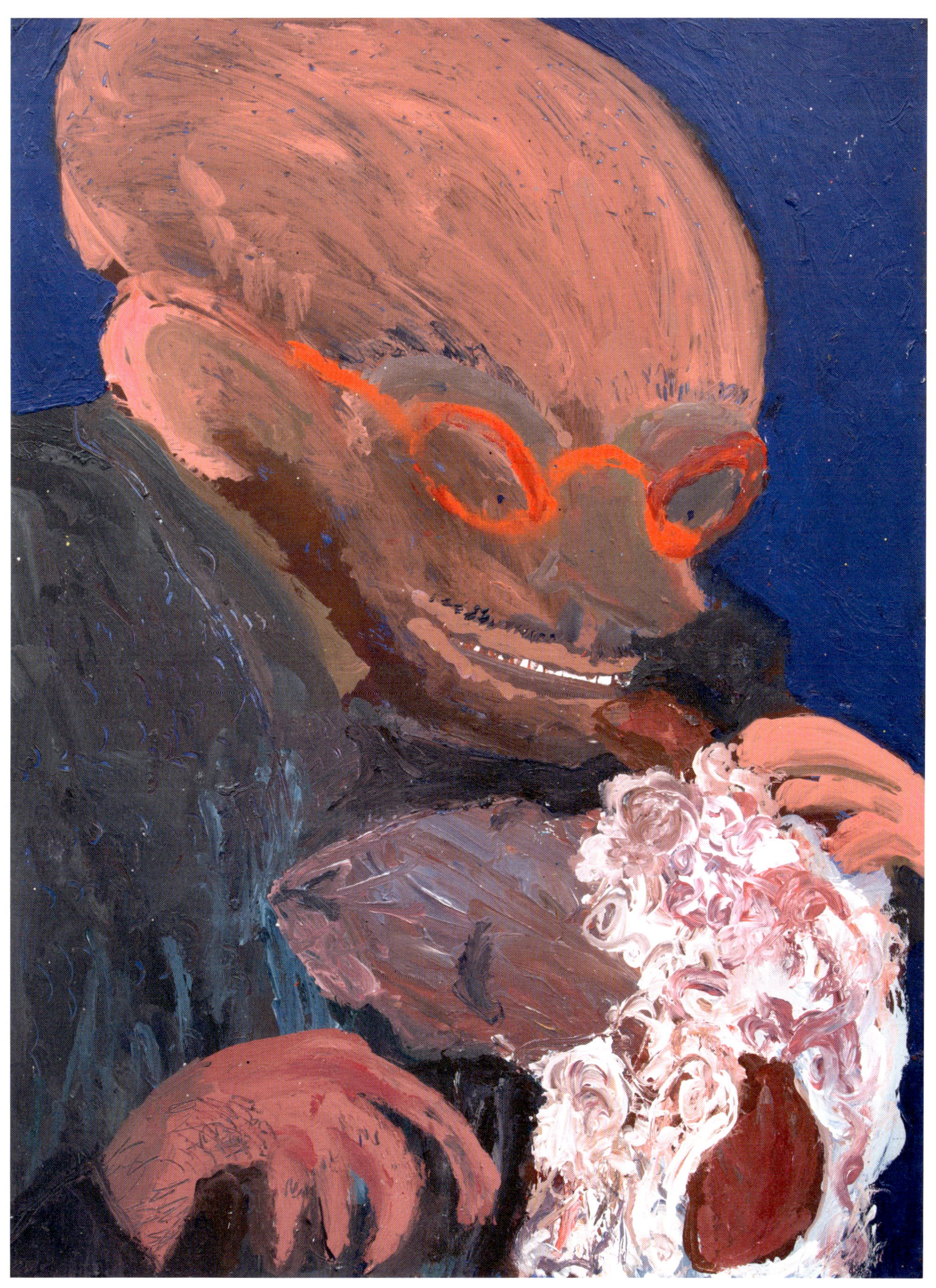

Untitled (Self-Portrait), 1982
Acrylic on found paper board
27 × 20¼ inches (68.6 × 51.4 cm)

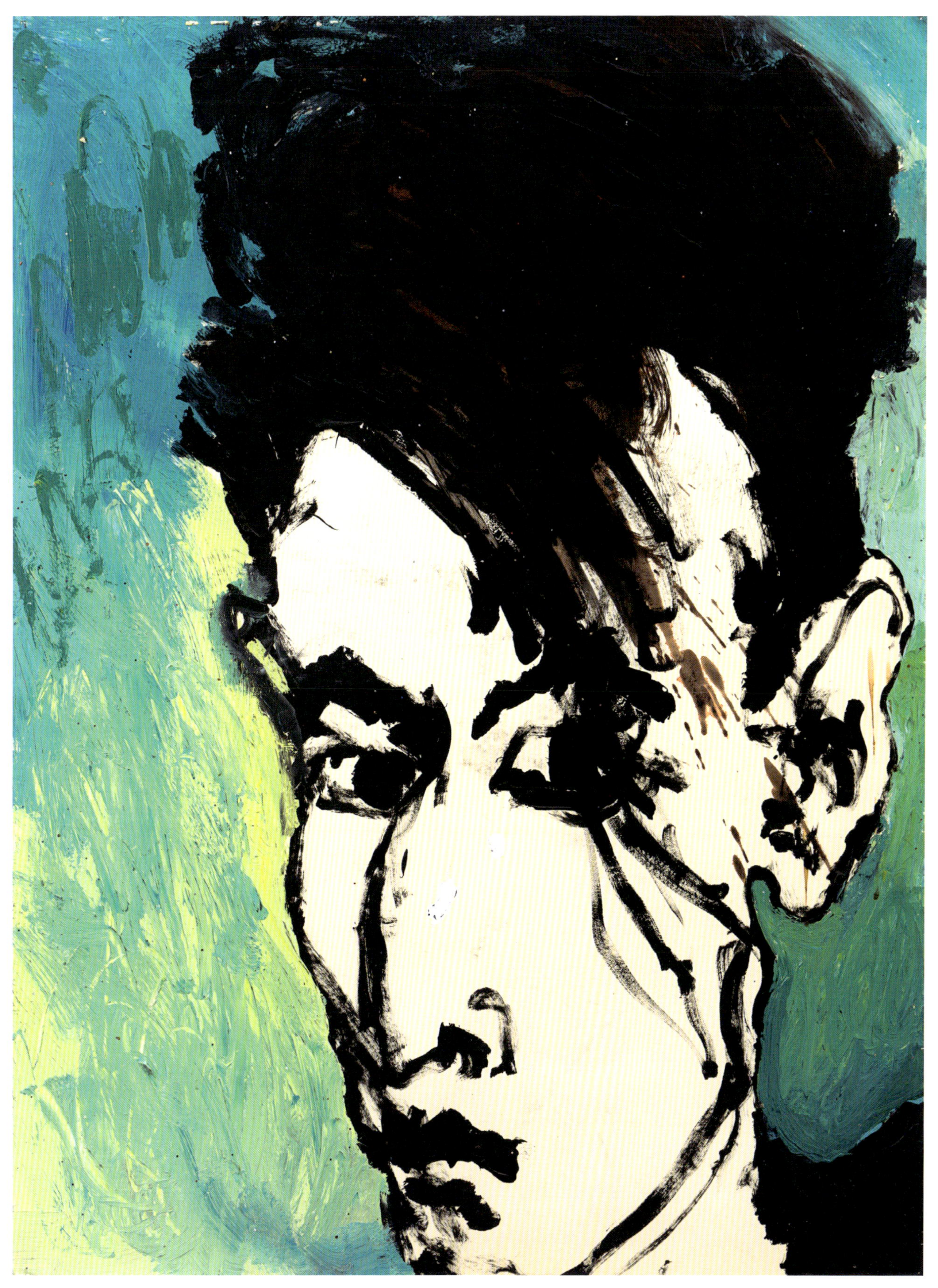

Self-Portrait with Platinum Hair, 1982
Acrylic on found paper board
24 × 19 inches (61 × 48.3 cm)

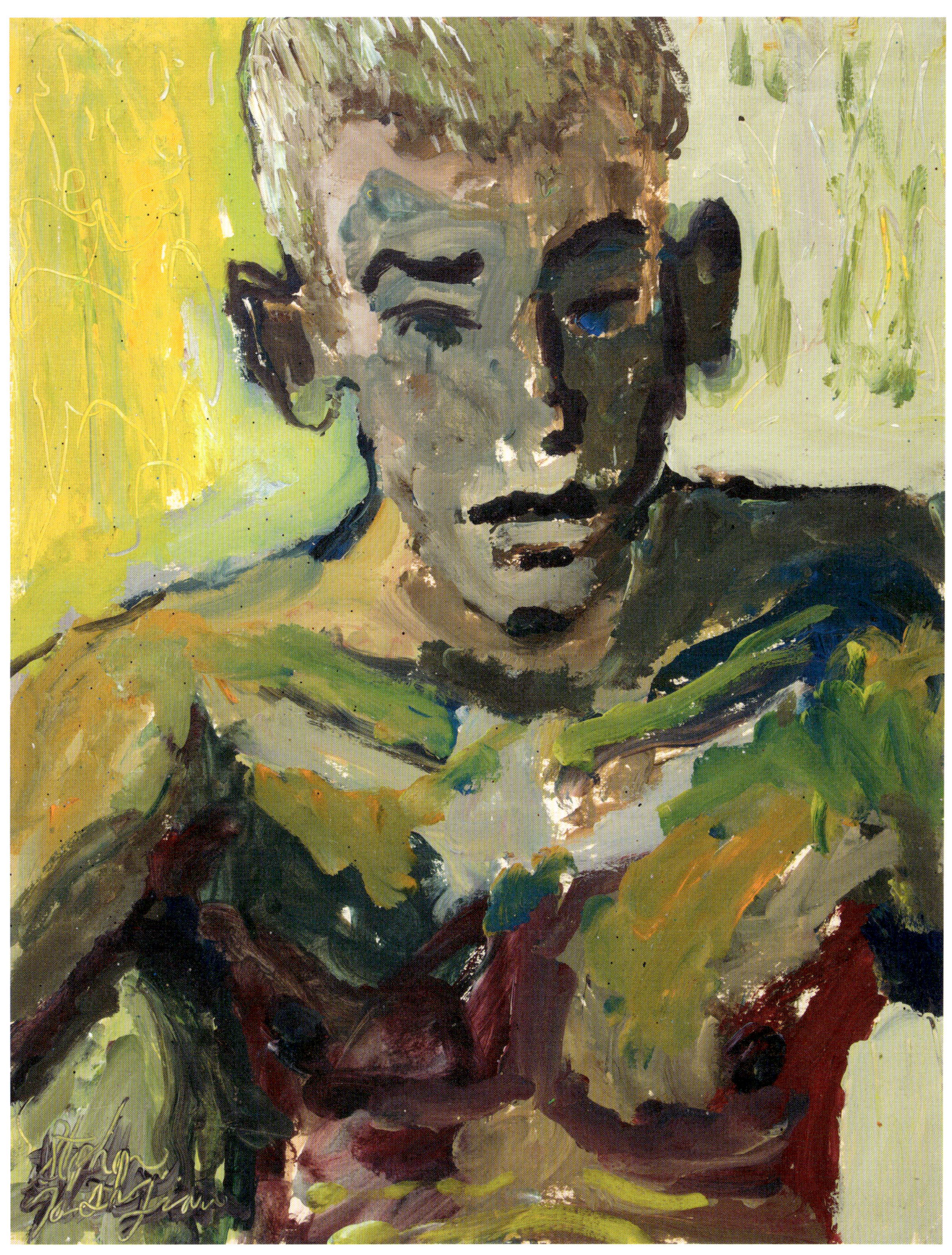

Untitled (Self-Portrait), 1985
Acrylic on canvas
62 × 52 inches (157.5 × 132.1 cm)

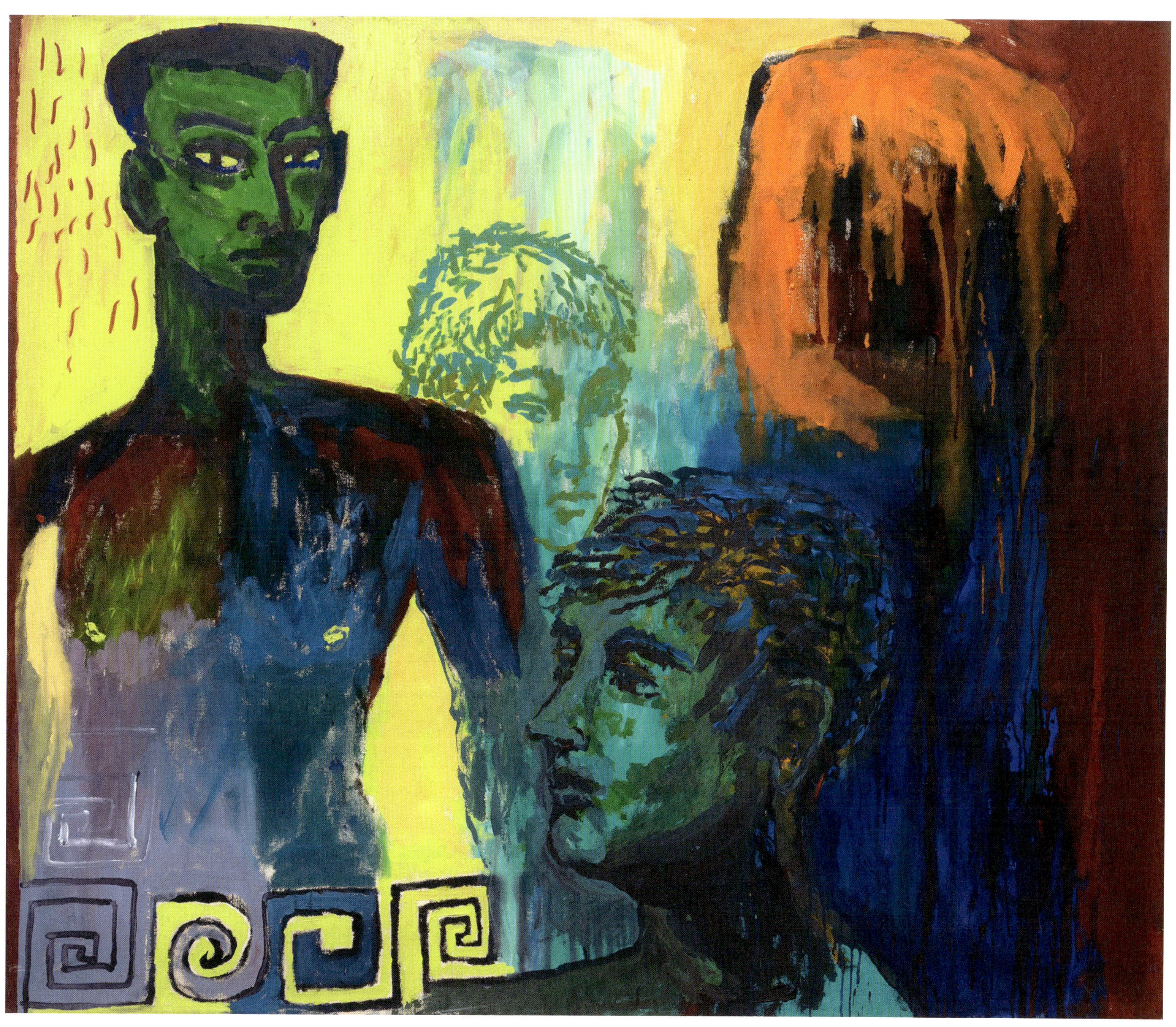

Classical Beauty, 1984
Acrylic on canvas
48 × 36 inches (121.9 × 91.4 cm)

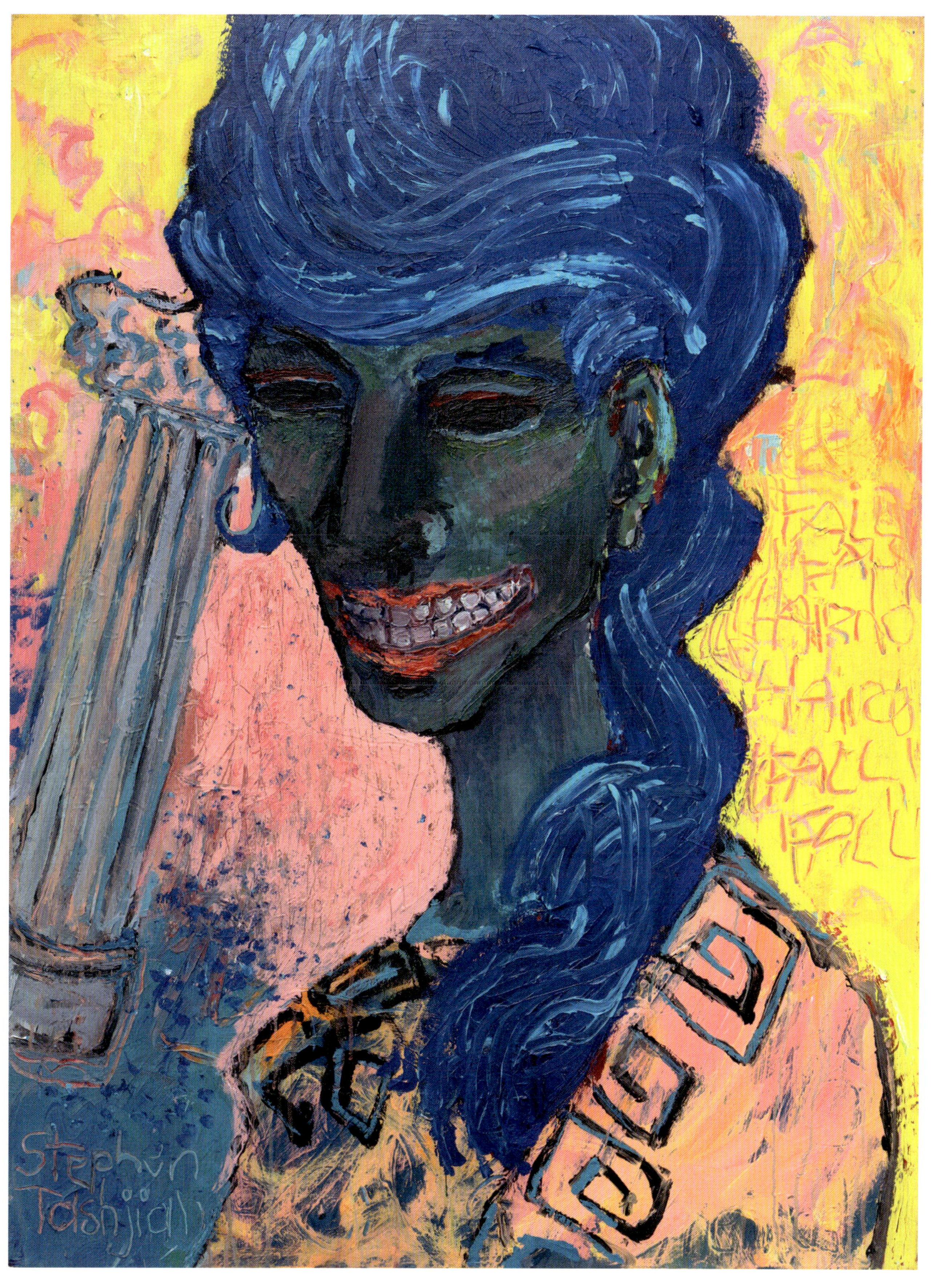
FALL
FALL
FALL
Stephen
Tashjian

Portrait of Clark Render
from the Green Dimension, 1986
Acrylic and glitter on canvas
58 × 38 inches (147.3 × 96.5 cm)

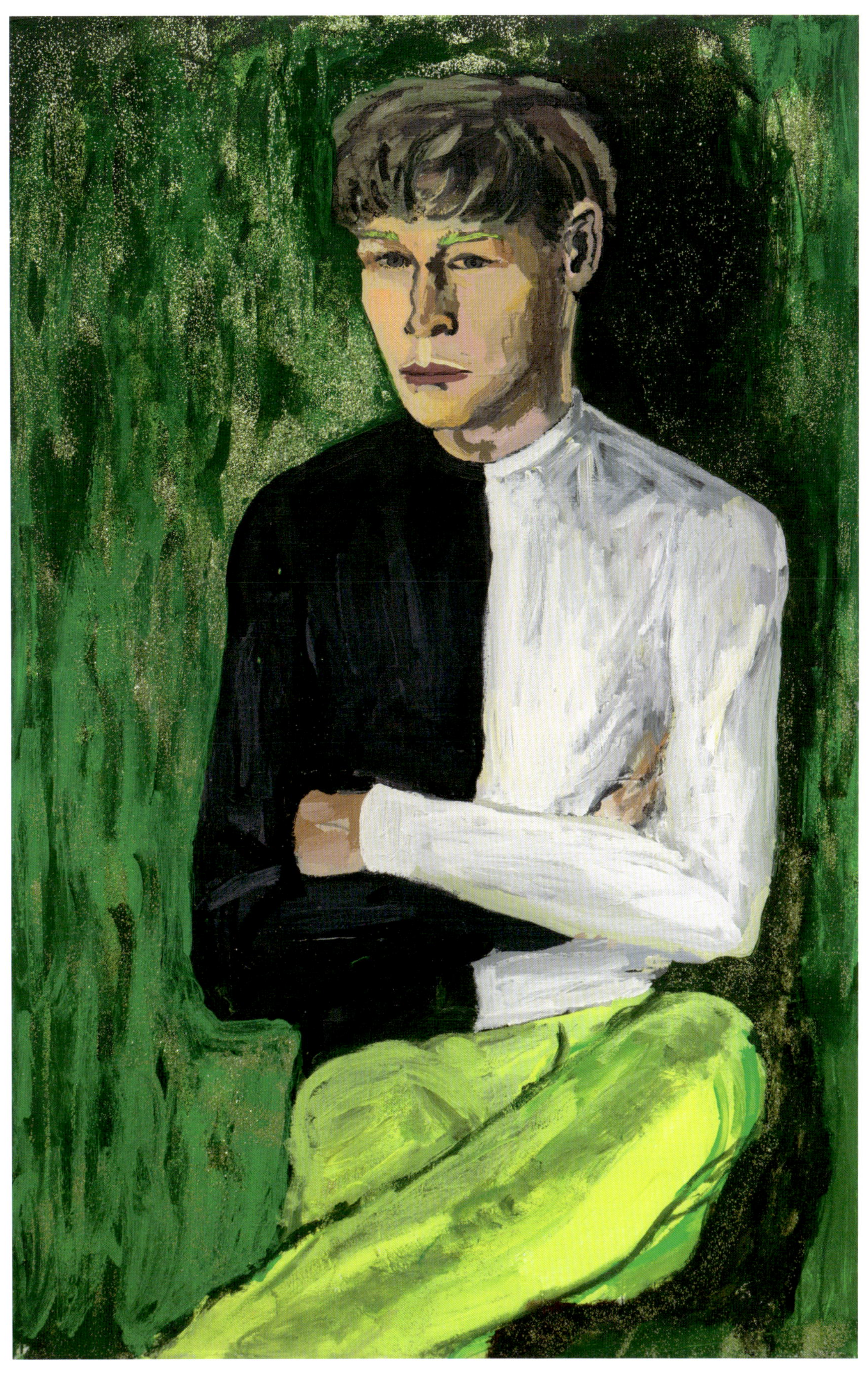

Mark Morrisroe, 1985
Acrylic on canvas
68 × 36 inches (172.7 × 91.4 cm)

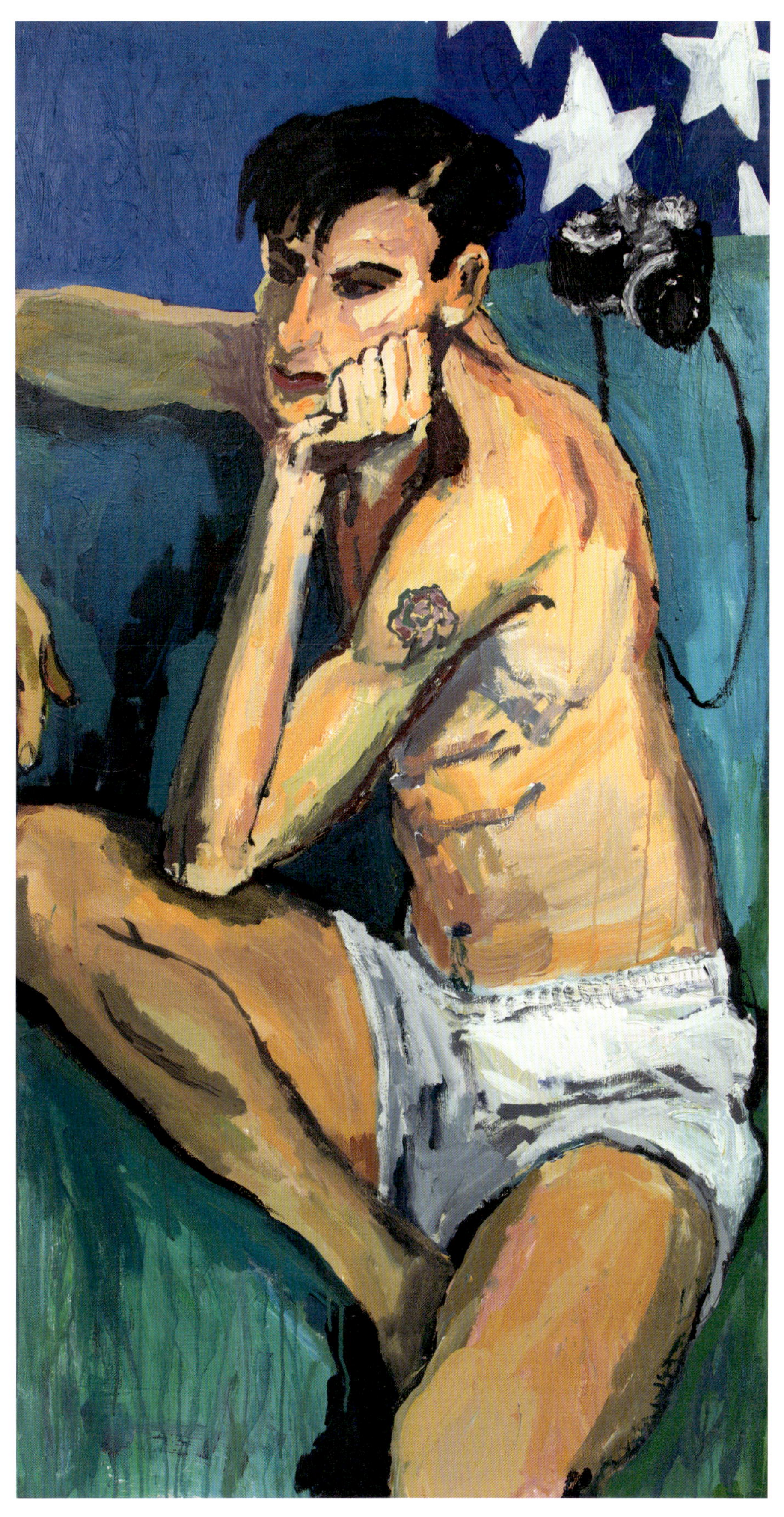

The Beautiful Ones, 1986
Acrylic and glitter on canvas
32¼ × 22¼ inches (81.9 × 56.5 cm)

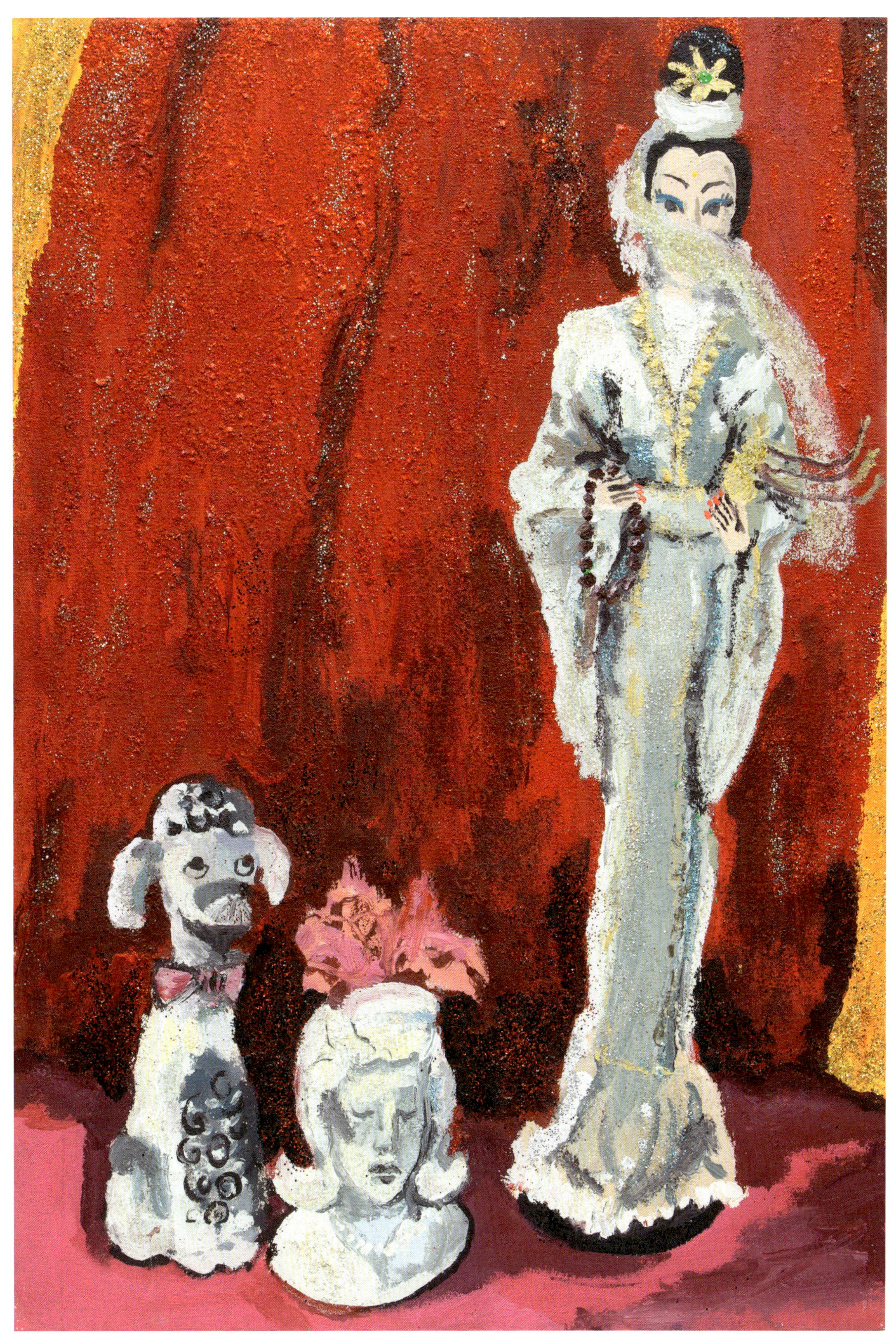

Vita-Chick, 1986
Acrylic and glitter on canvas
48¼ × 32 inches (122.6 × 81.3 cm)

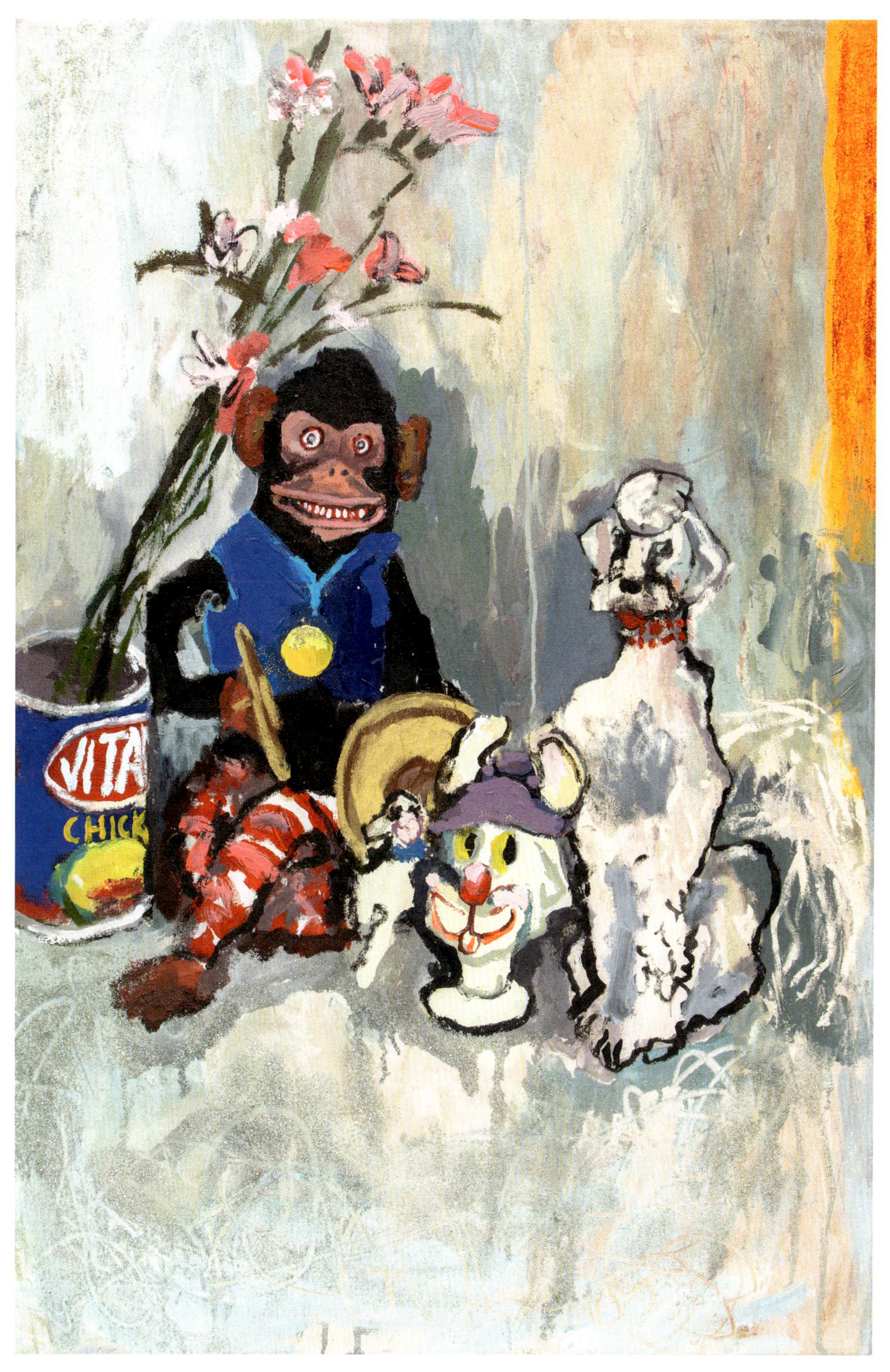
VITA
CHICK

Guido, 1986
Acrylic and glitter on canvas
78 × 48 inches (198.1 × 121.9 cm)

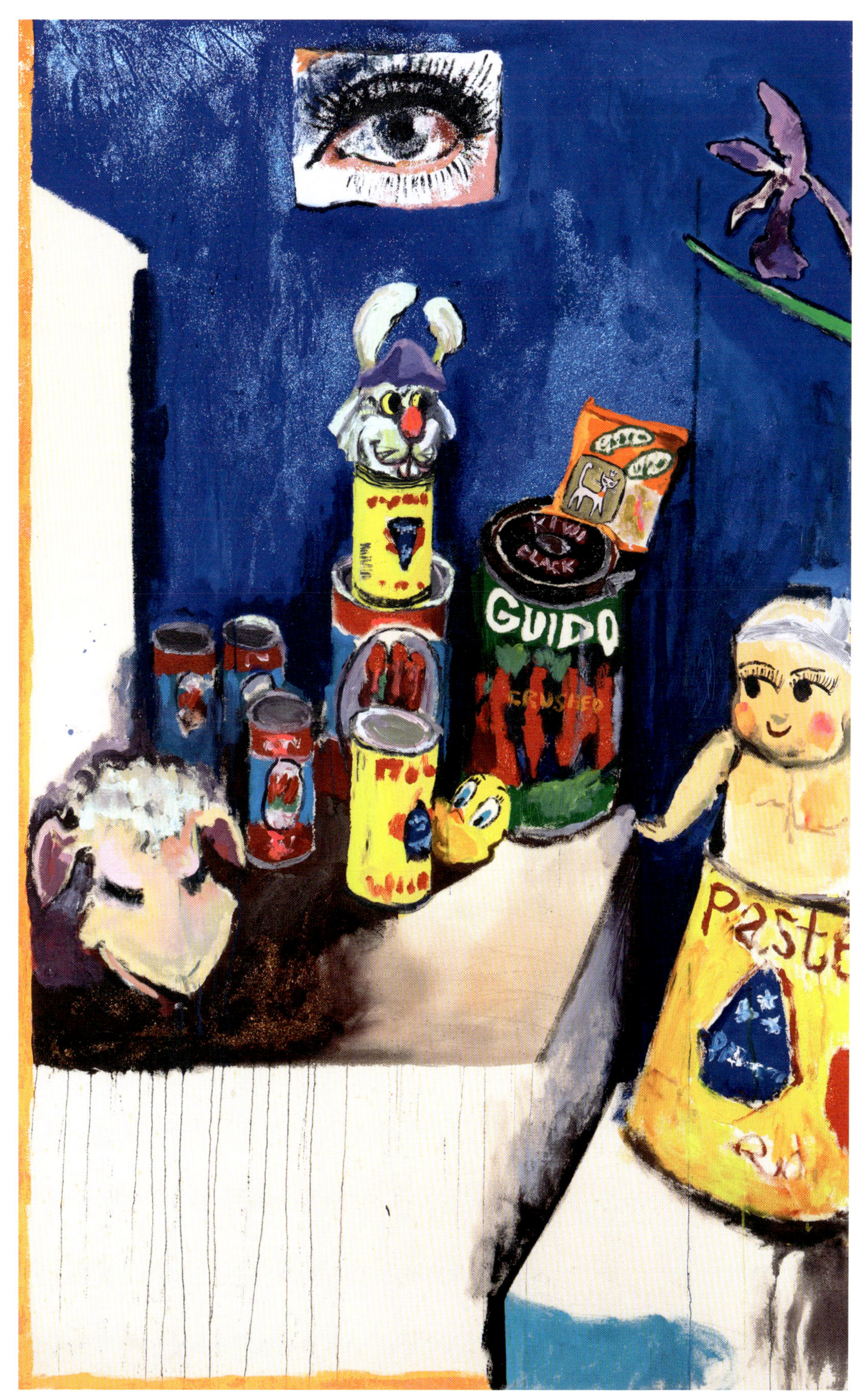
KIWI
BLACK
GUIDO
Paste

You Can Only Get It in New York, 1986
Acrylic and glitter on canvas
52 × 38½ inches (132.1 × 97.8 cm)

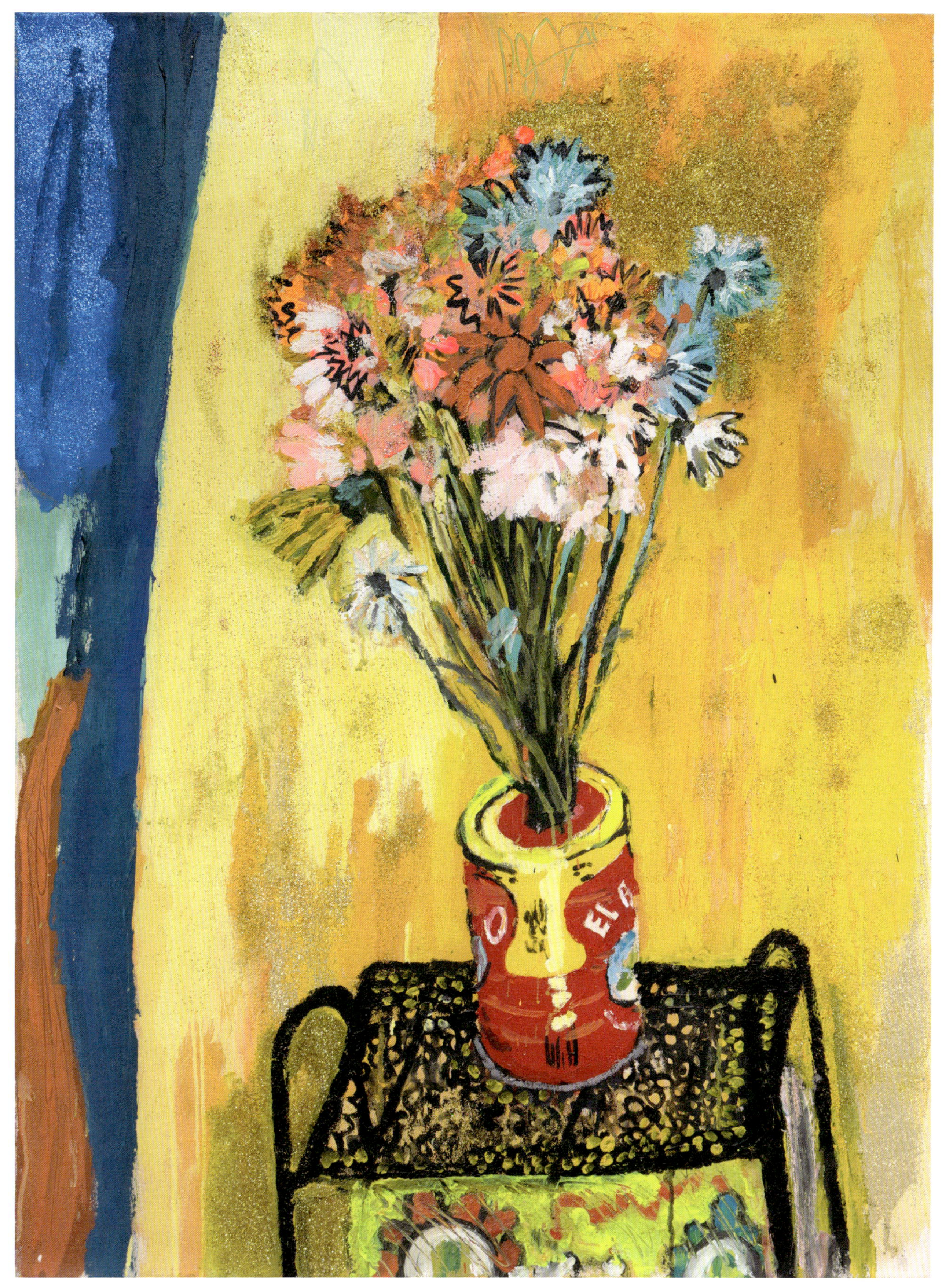

Untitled (Self-Portrait), 1982
Crayon and acrylic on paper
11 × 8½ inches (27.9 × 21.6 cm)

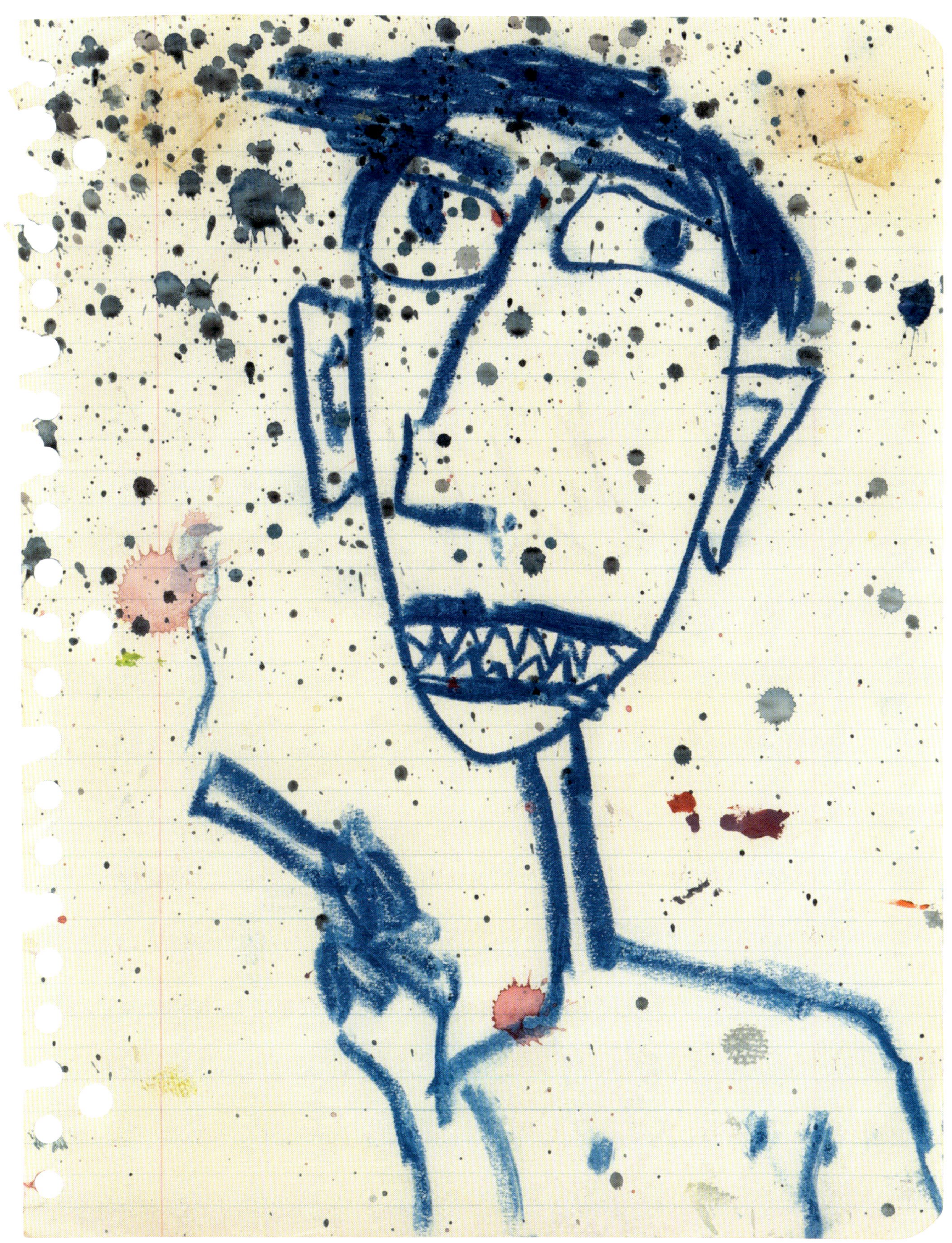

Untitled, 1987
Acrylic and glitter on paper
22 × 30 inches (55.9 × 76.2 cm)

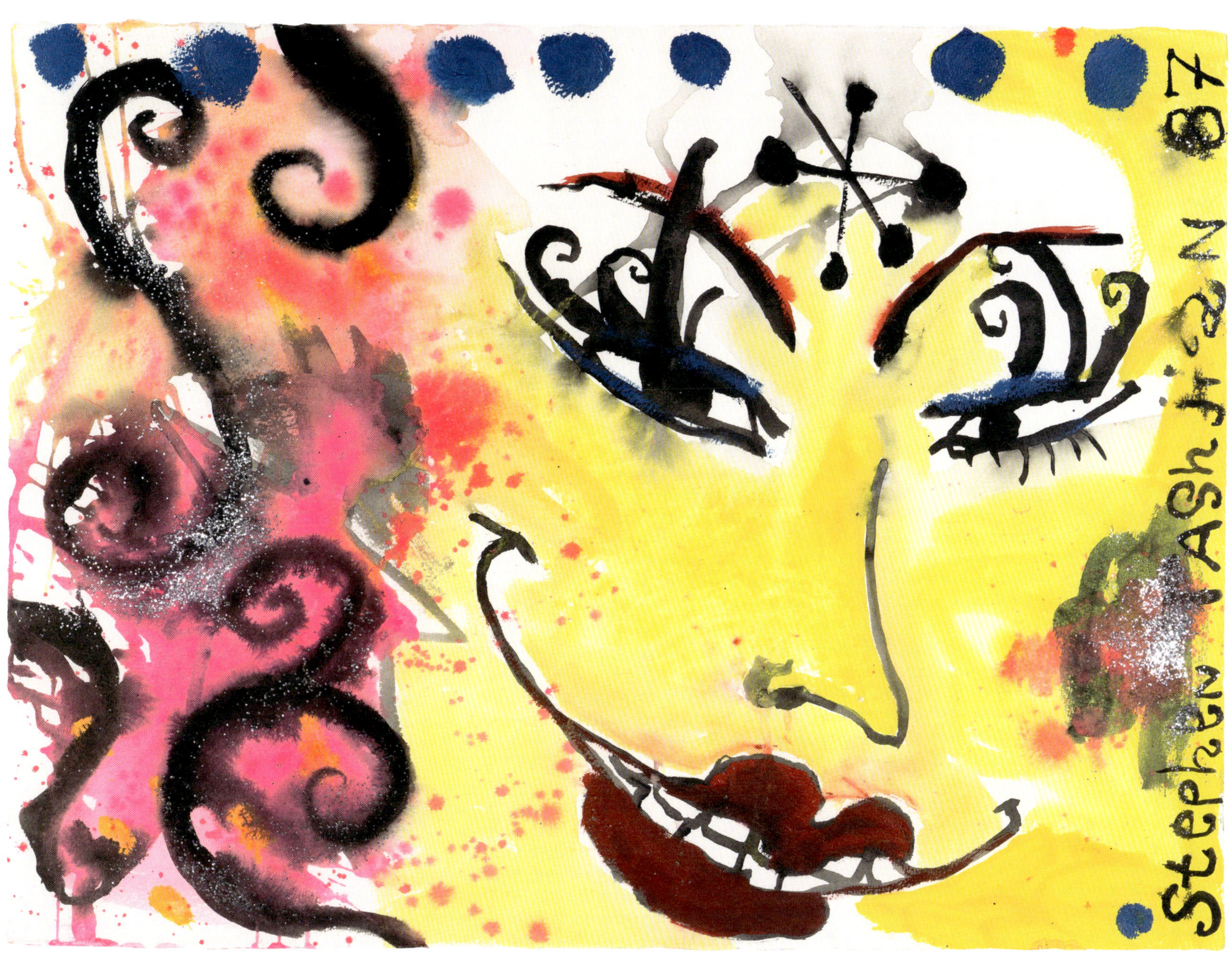

Yes, 1984
Acrylic and glitter on paper
39¼ × 27½ inches (99.7 × 69.9 cm)

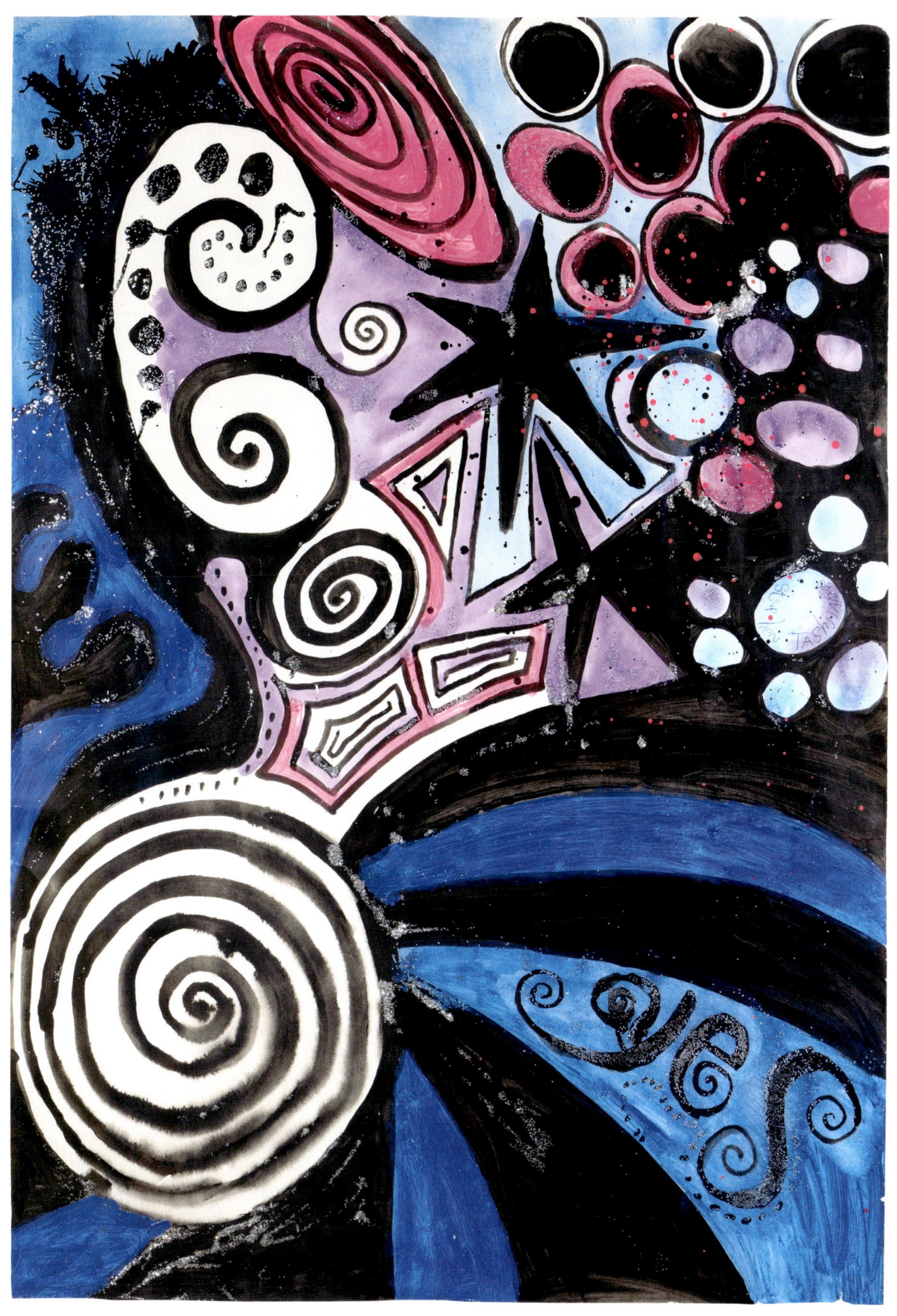

Untitled, 1988
Acrylic on paper
30 × 22¾ inches (76.2 × 57.8 cm)

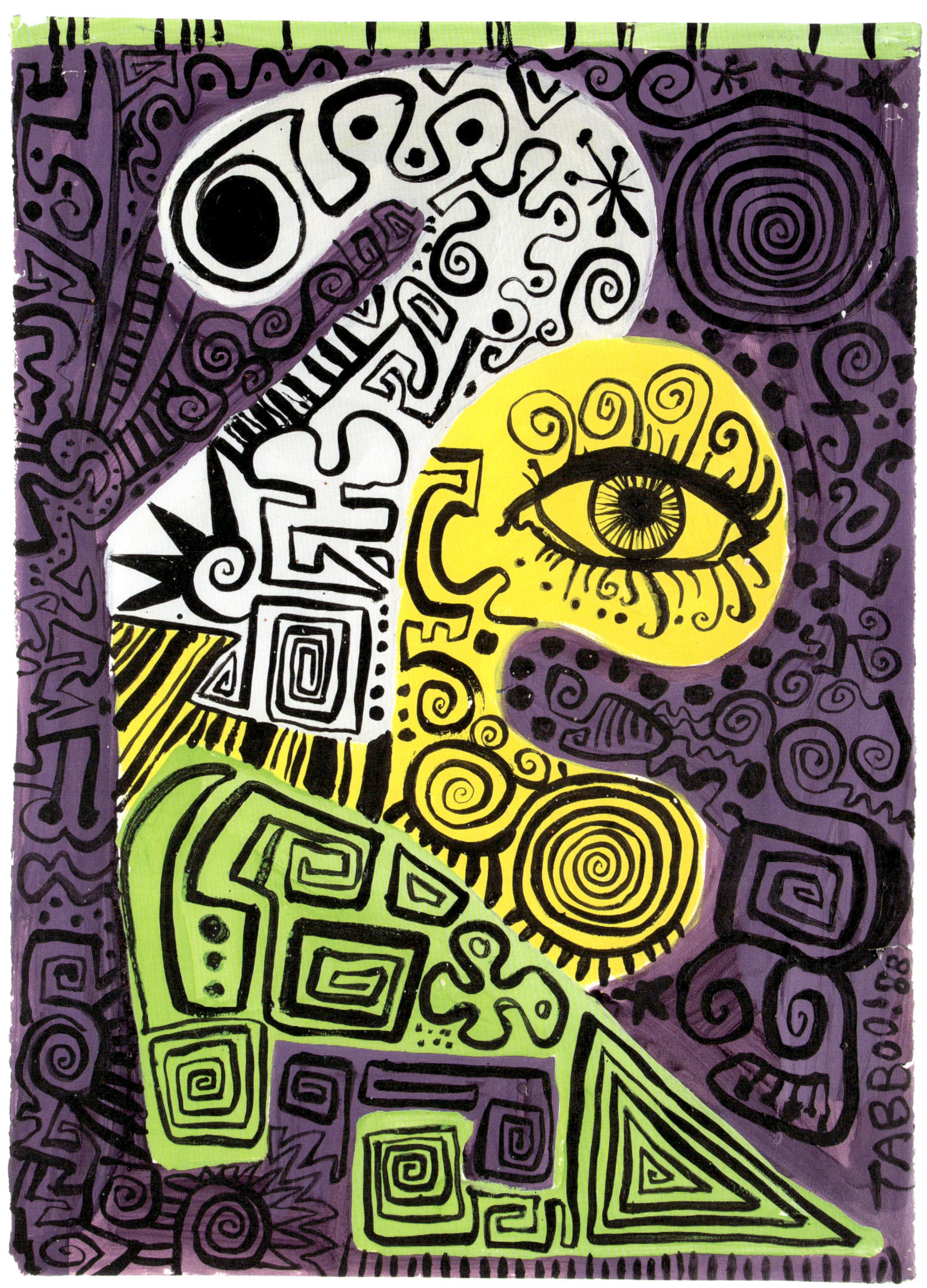
TABBOO! '88

Untitled, 1986
Acrylic and glitter on paper
39 × 27 inches (99.1 × 68.6 cm)

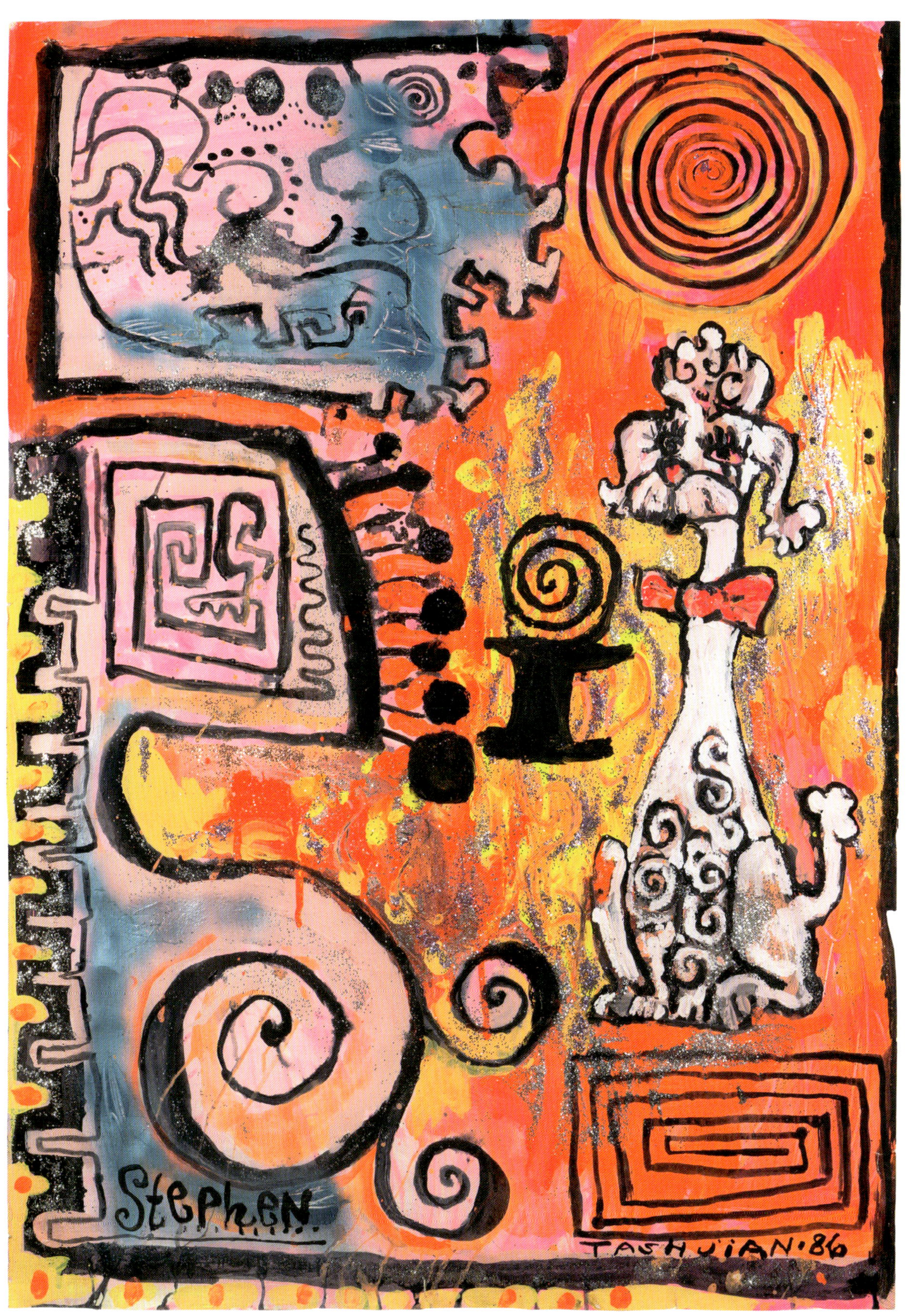
Stephen
TASHJIAN·86

Untitled, 1988
Acrylic and glitter on paper
30 × 22 inches (76.2 × 55.9 cm)

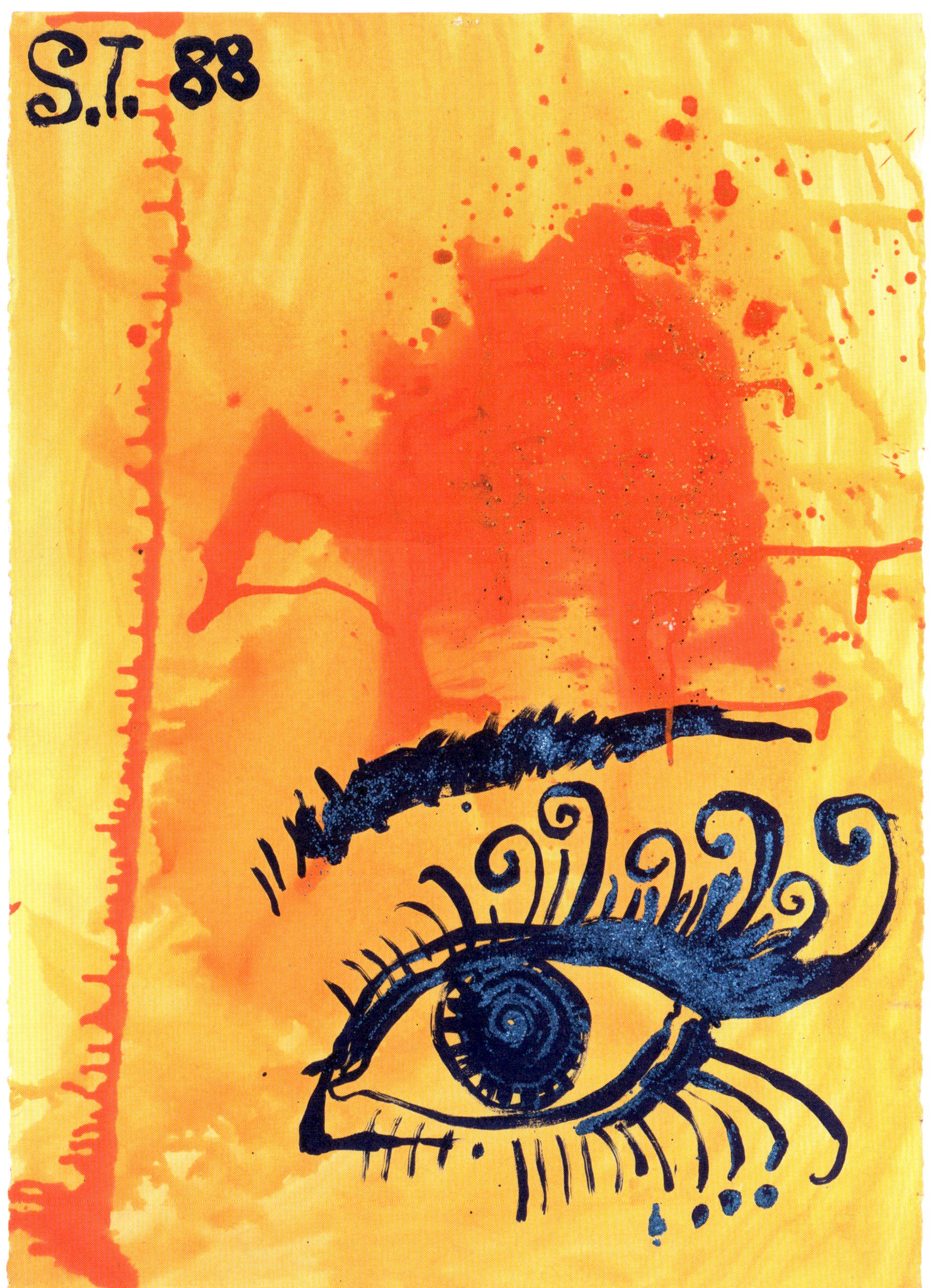
S.T. 88

Untitled, ca. 1988
Acrylic and collage on paper
29¾ × 22¼ inches (75.6 × 56.5 cm)

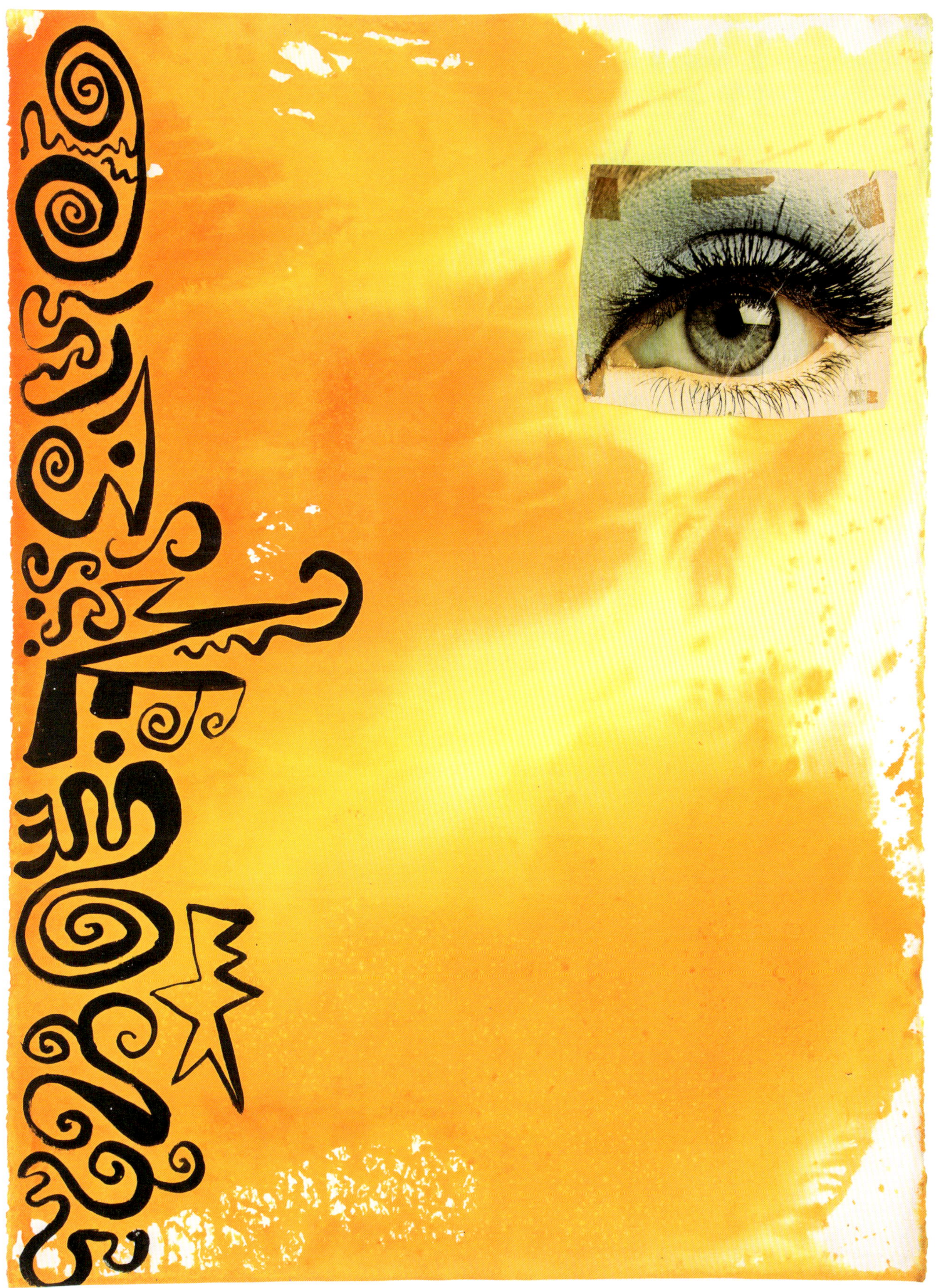

Transendental Unconditional Love, 1986
Acrylic and glitter on paper
30 × 23 inches (76.2 × 58.4 cm)

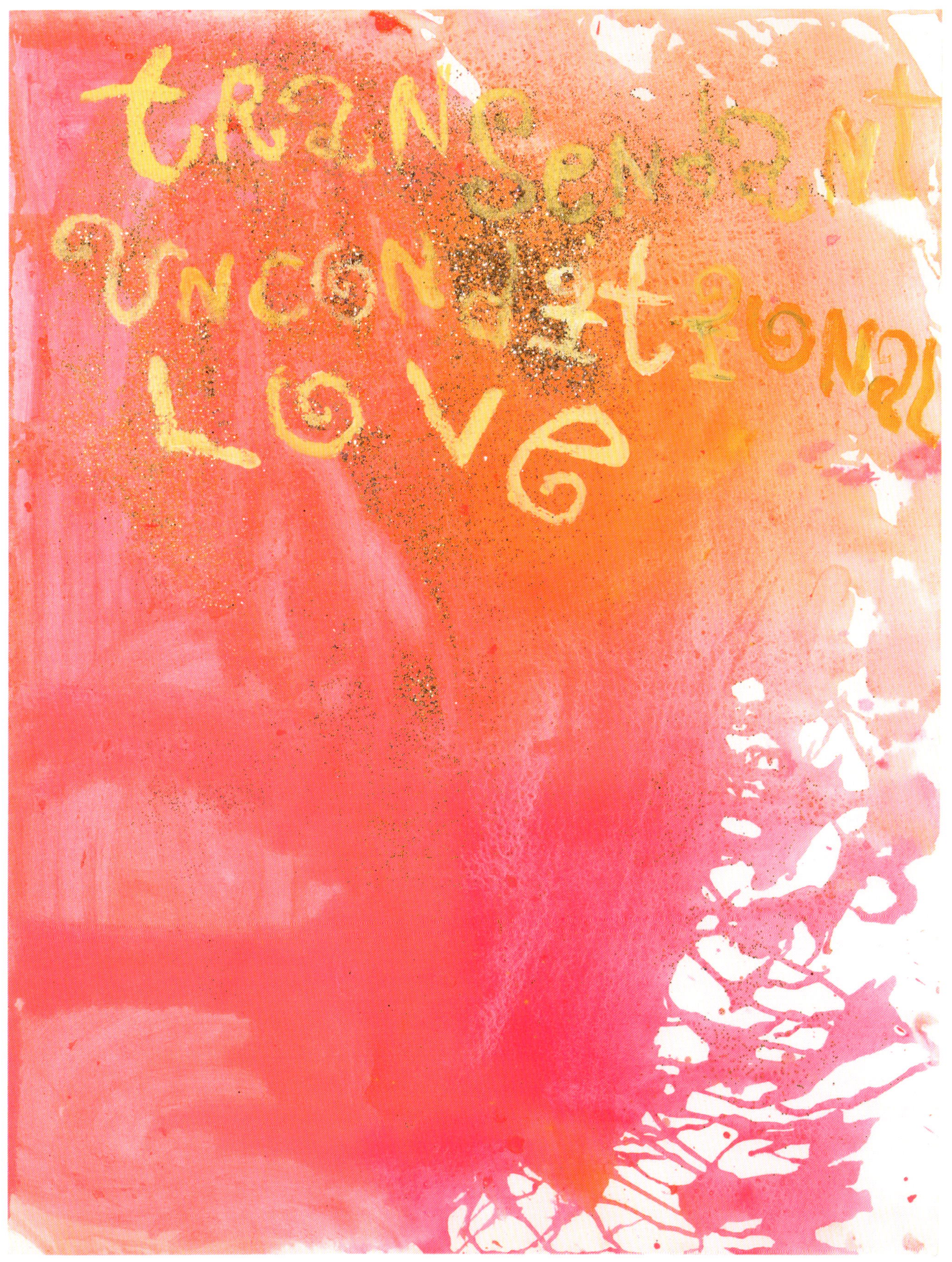
transcendant
unconditional
LOVE

Untitled, n.d.
Acrylic on paper
30 × 22 inches (76.2 × 55.9 cm)

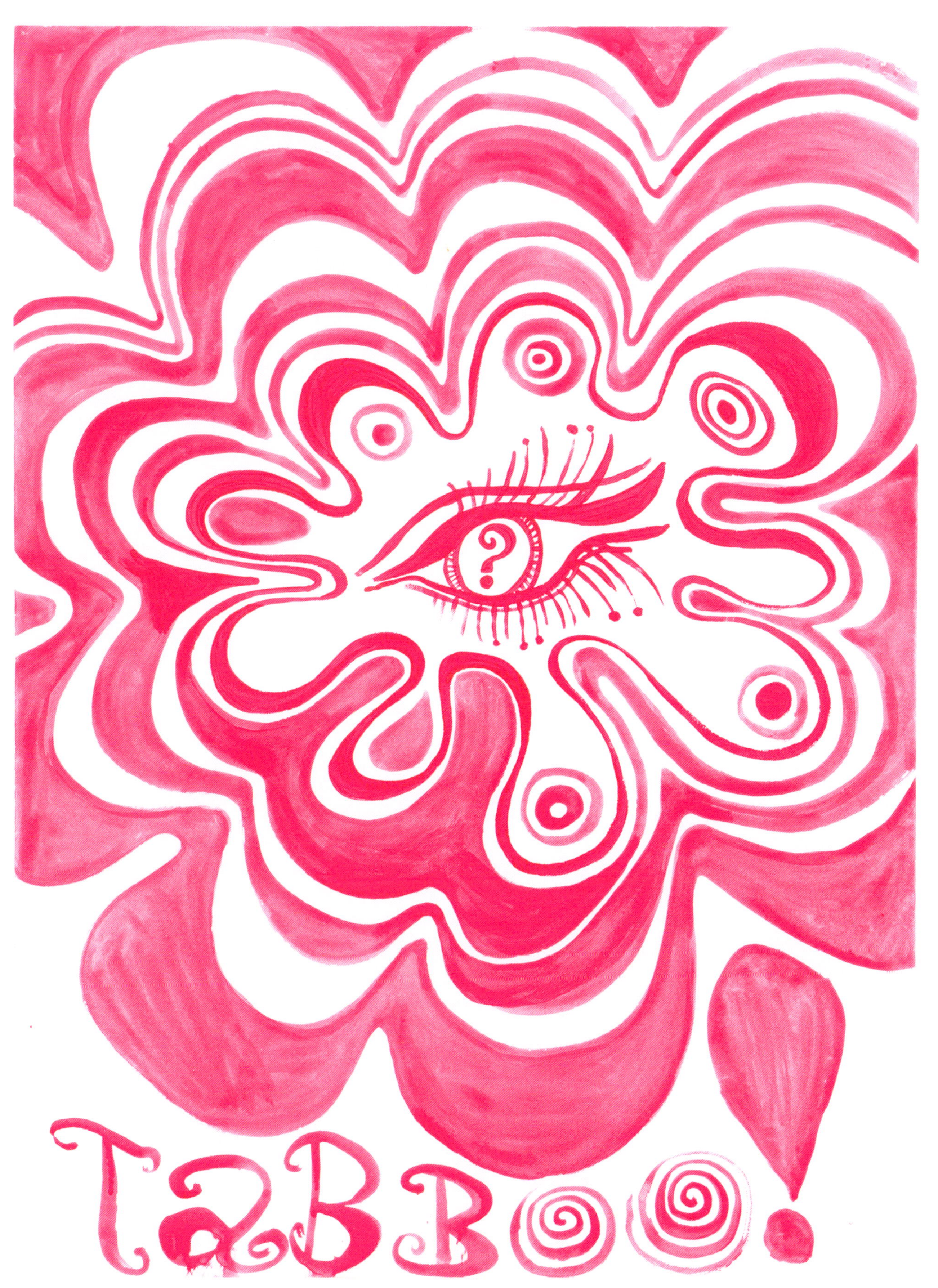
TaBBoo!

Sally Bowles, 1982
Acrylic on found paper
35 × 47½ inches (88.9 × 120.7 cm)

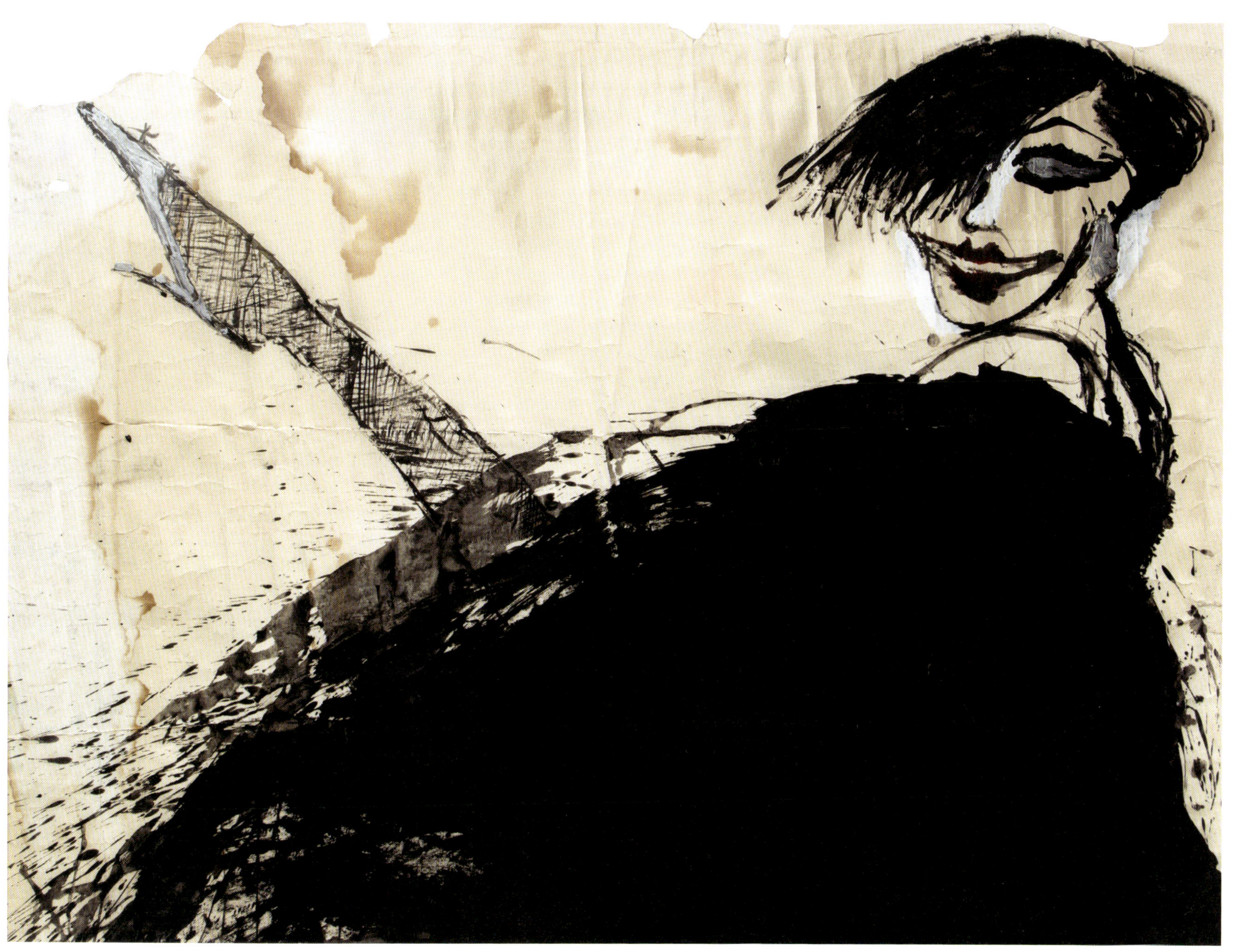

Self-Portrait, n.d.
Acrylic on paper
30 × 22 inches (76.2 × 55.9 cm)

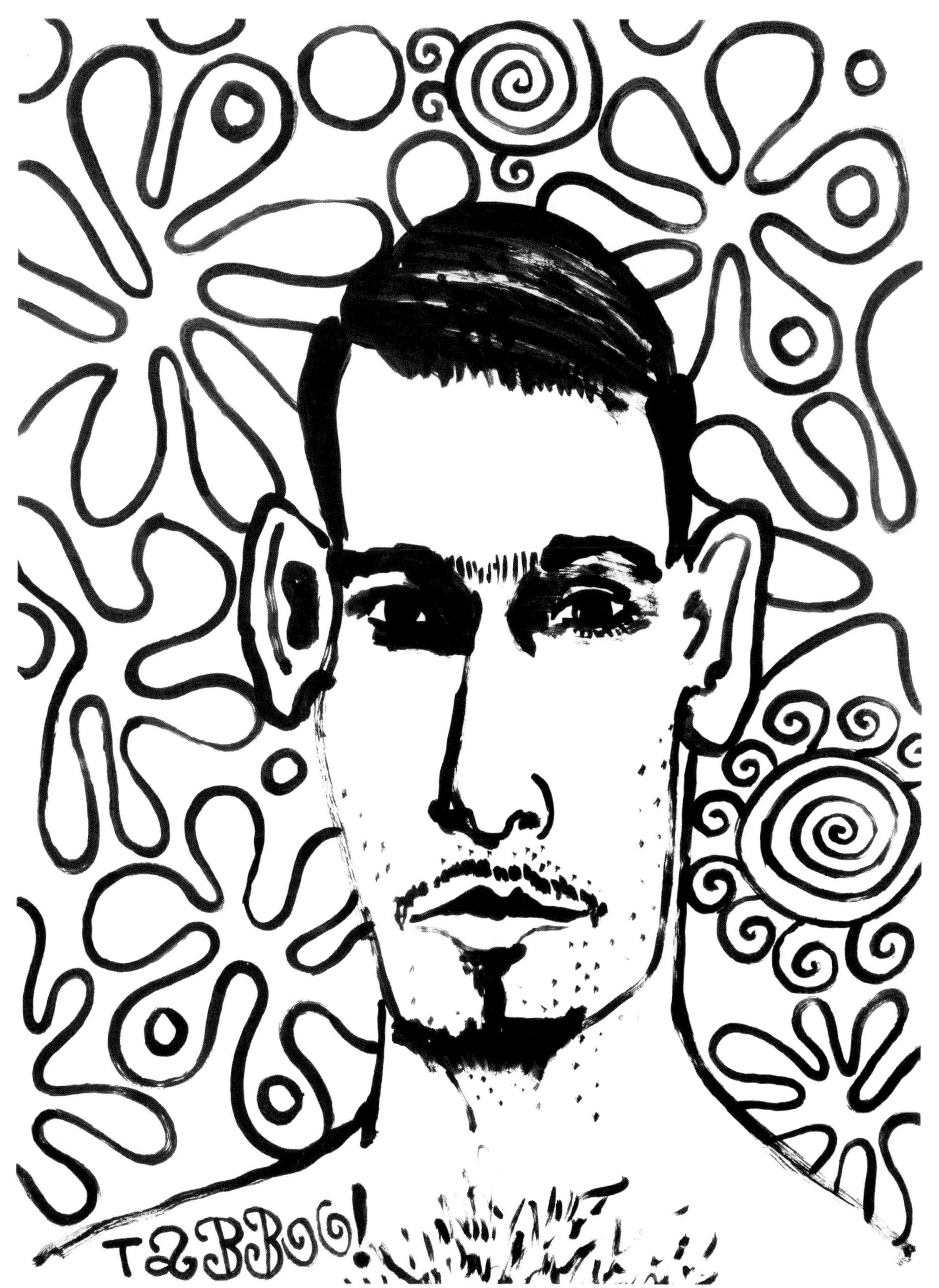
TABBOO!

Pyramid Figure (Phillip Forrest), 1985
Acrylic on paper
14¼ × 5¾ inches (36.2 × 14.6 cm)

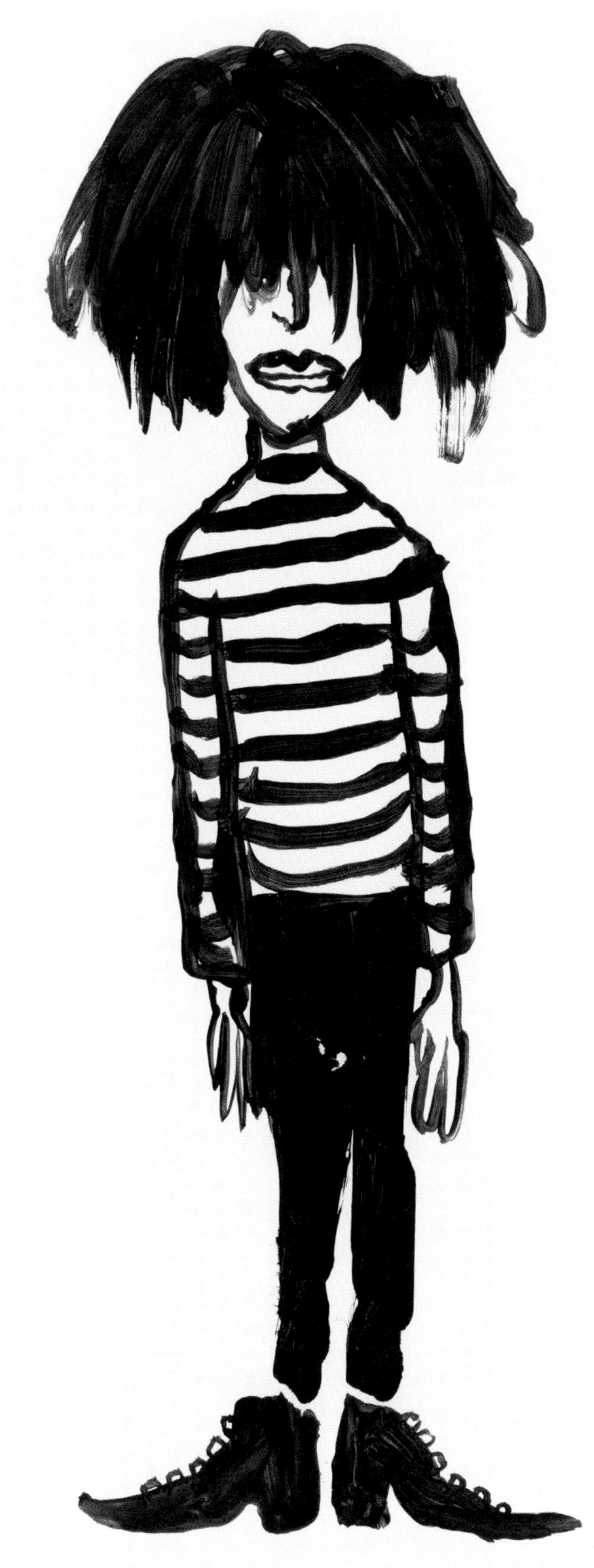

Three Pyramid Figures, 1985
Acrylic and collage on paper
28¼ × 21½ inches (71.8 × 54.6 cm)

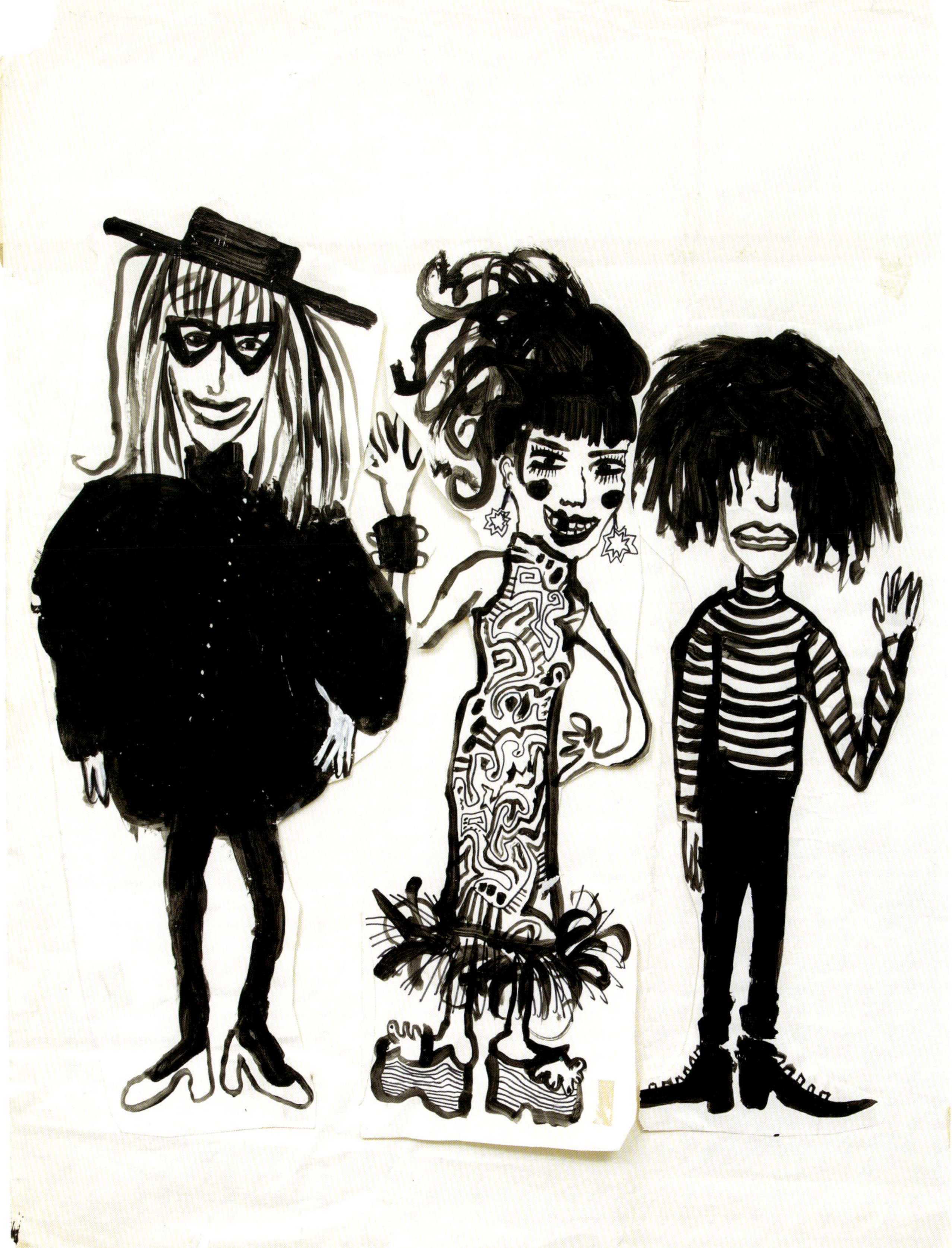

Thief of Bagdad (II), 1985
Acrylic on paper
27¾ × 39½ inches (70.5 × 100.3 cm)

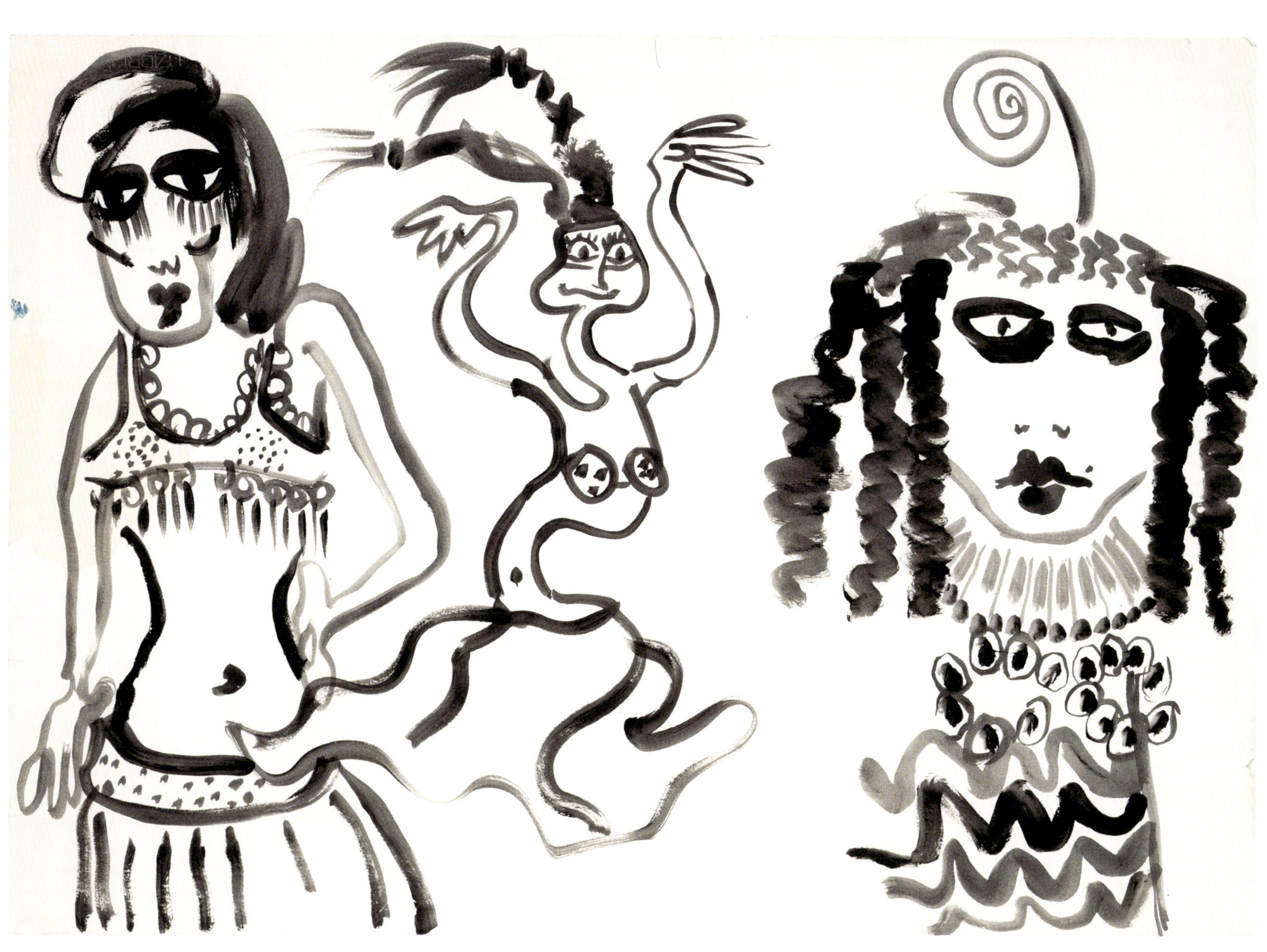

Untitled, ca. 1985
Acrylic and glitter on paper
24 × 35 inches (61 × 88.9 cm)

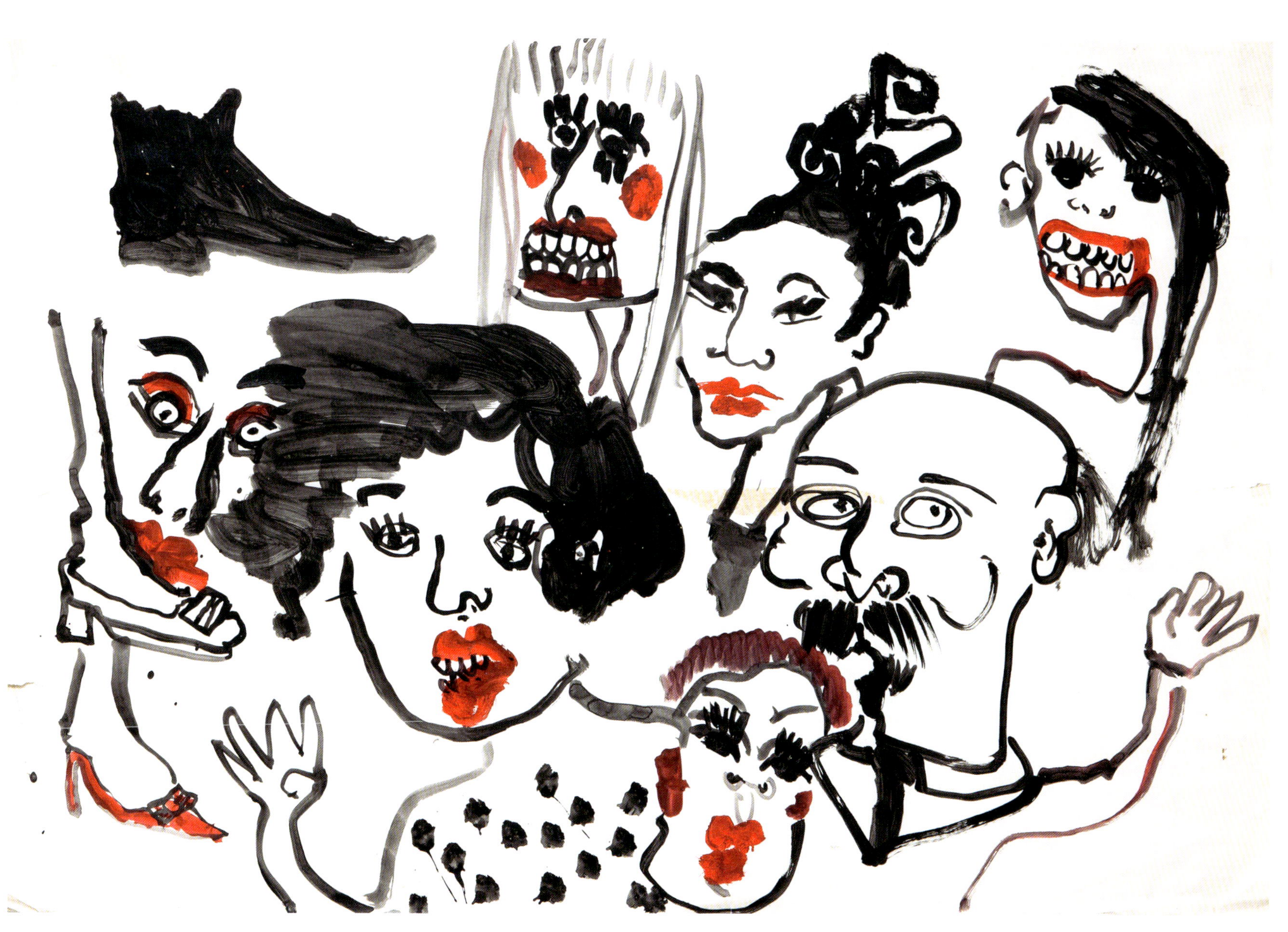

Untitled, ca. 1985
Acrylic and collage on paper
36 × 24 inches (91.4 × 61 cm)

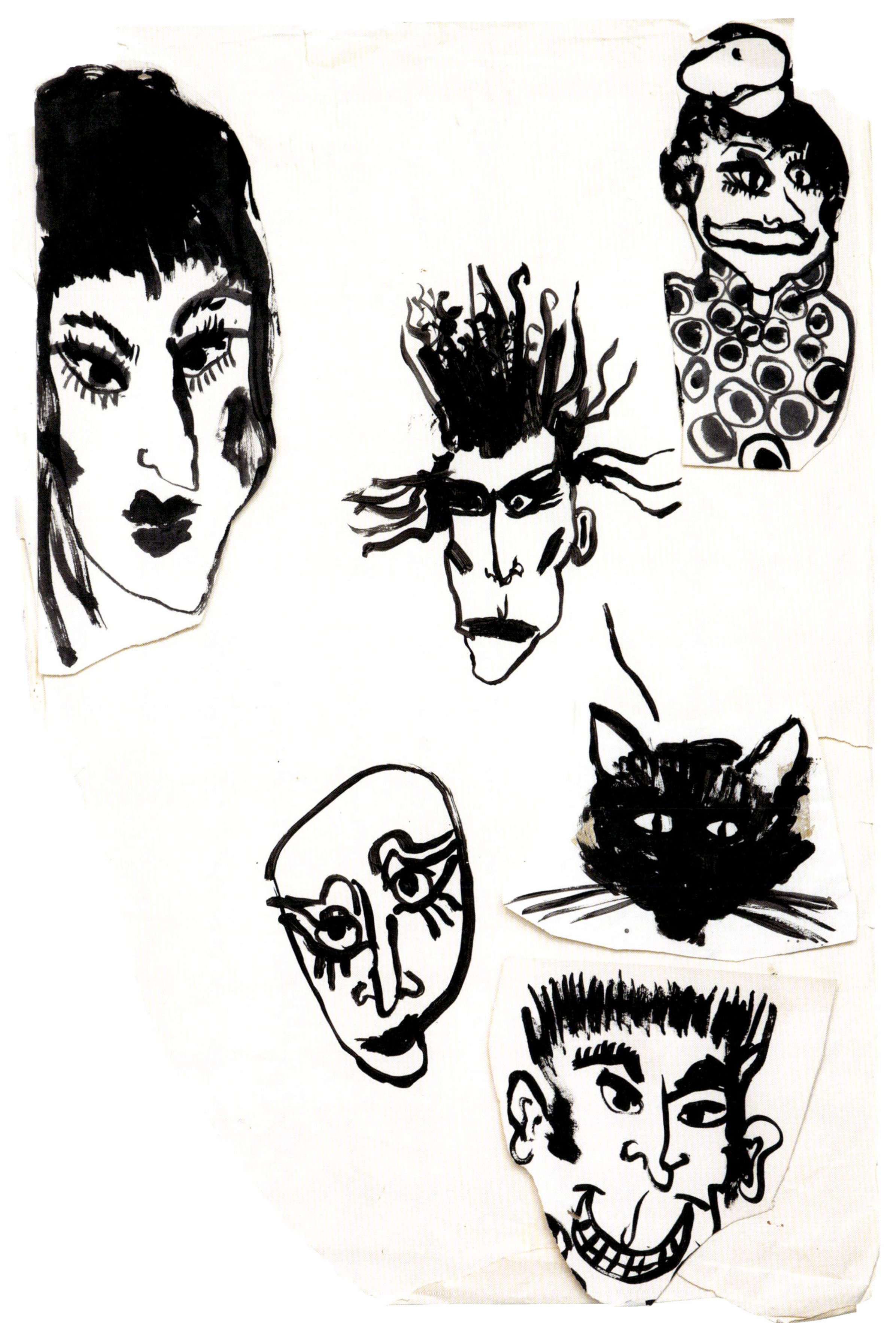

Psychedelic Mushroom Freak, 1985
Acrylic on paper
26 × 25½ inches (66 × 64.8 cm)

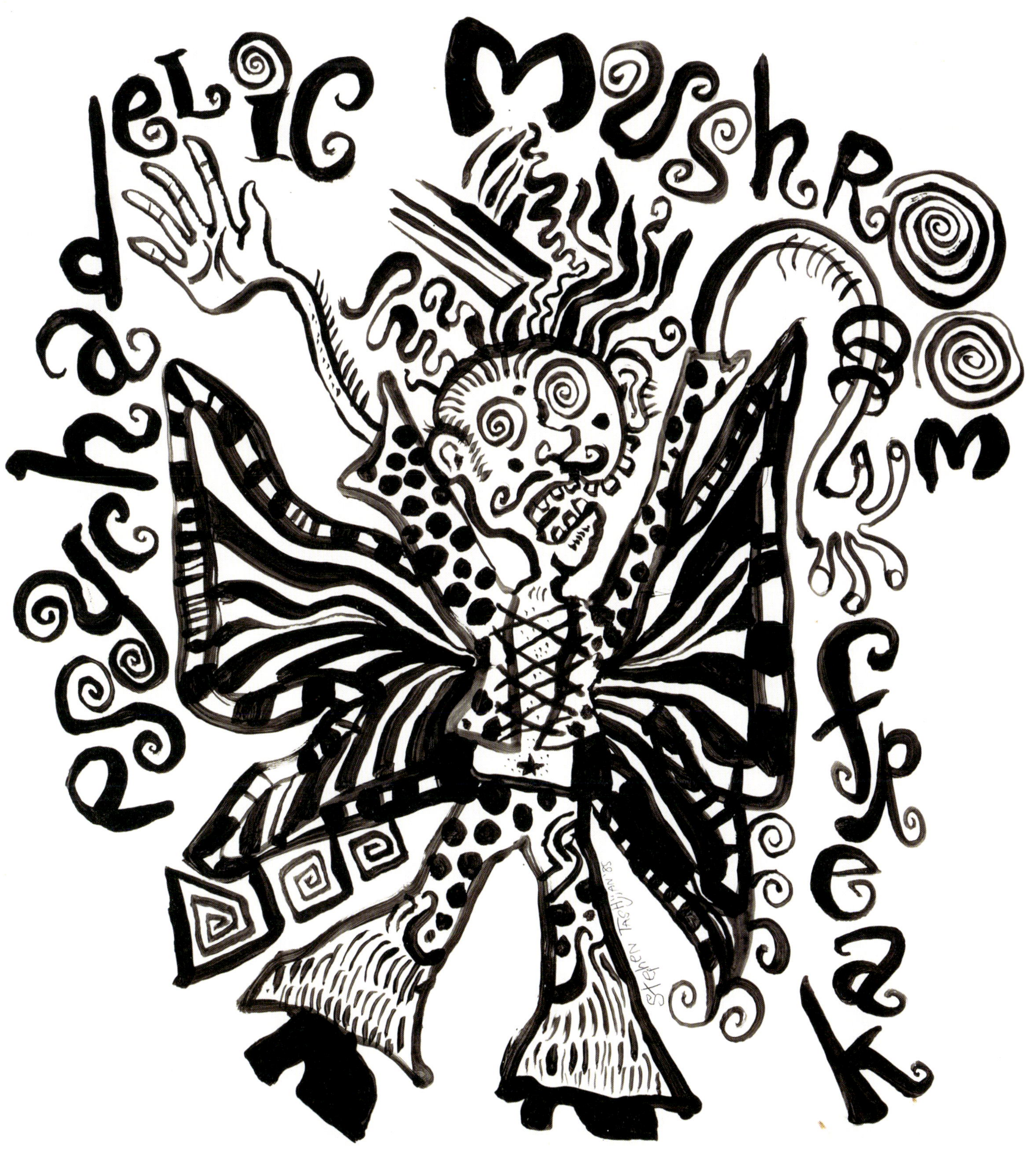
psychedelic mushroom freak
Stephen Tashjian '85

Untitled (Devil Girl), ca. 1985
Acrylic on paper
24 × 18 inches (61 × 45.7 cm)

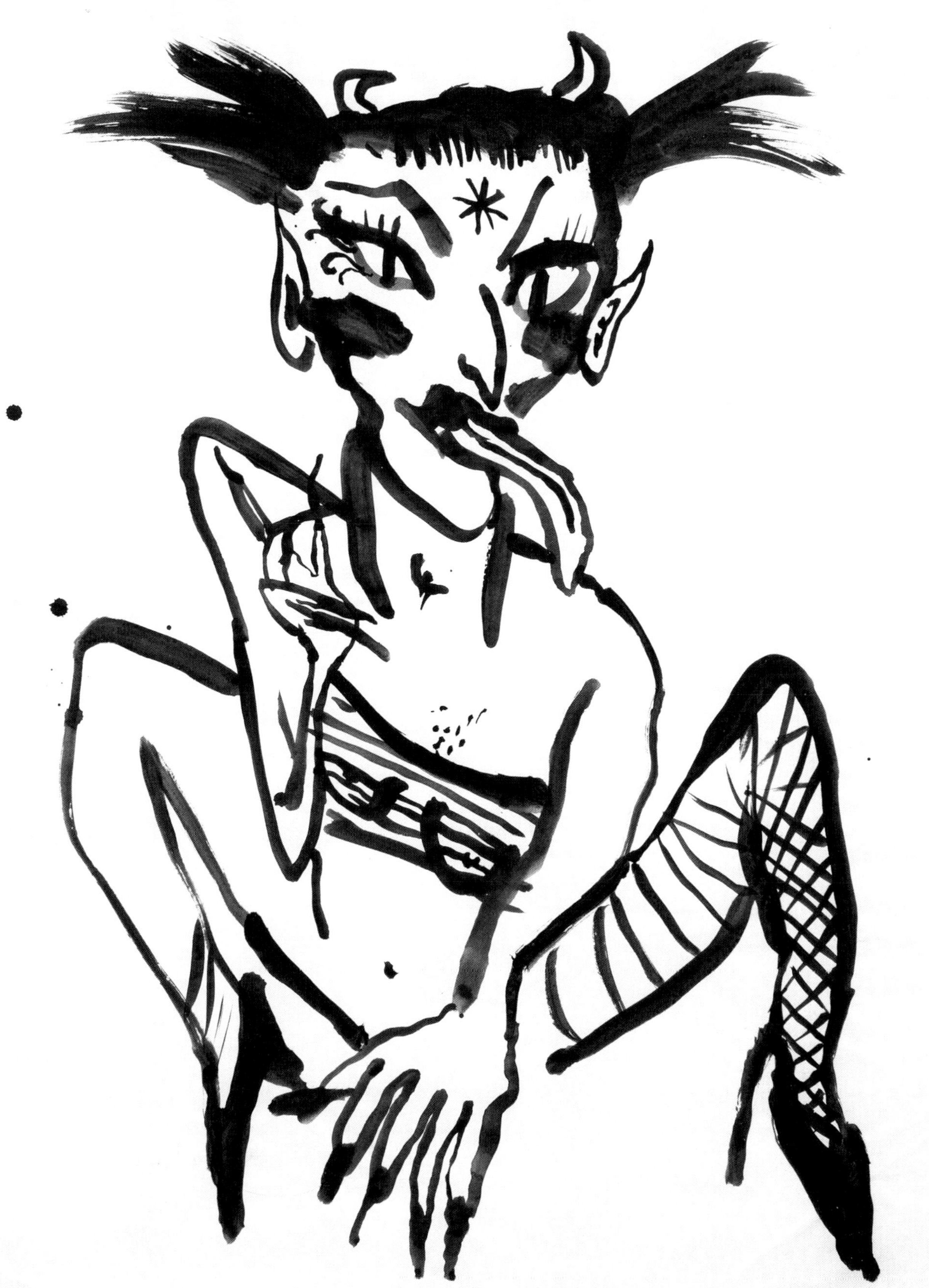

Alphabet, 1985
Acrylic and glitter on paper
39½ × 27¾ inches (100.3 × 70.5 cm)

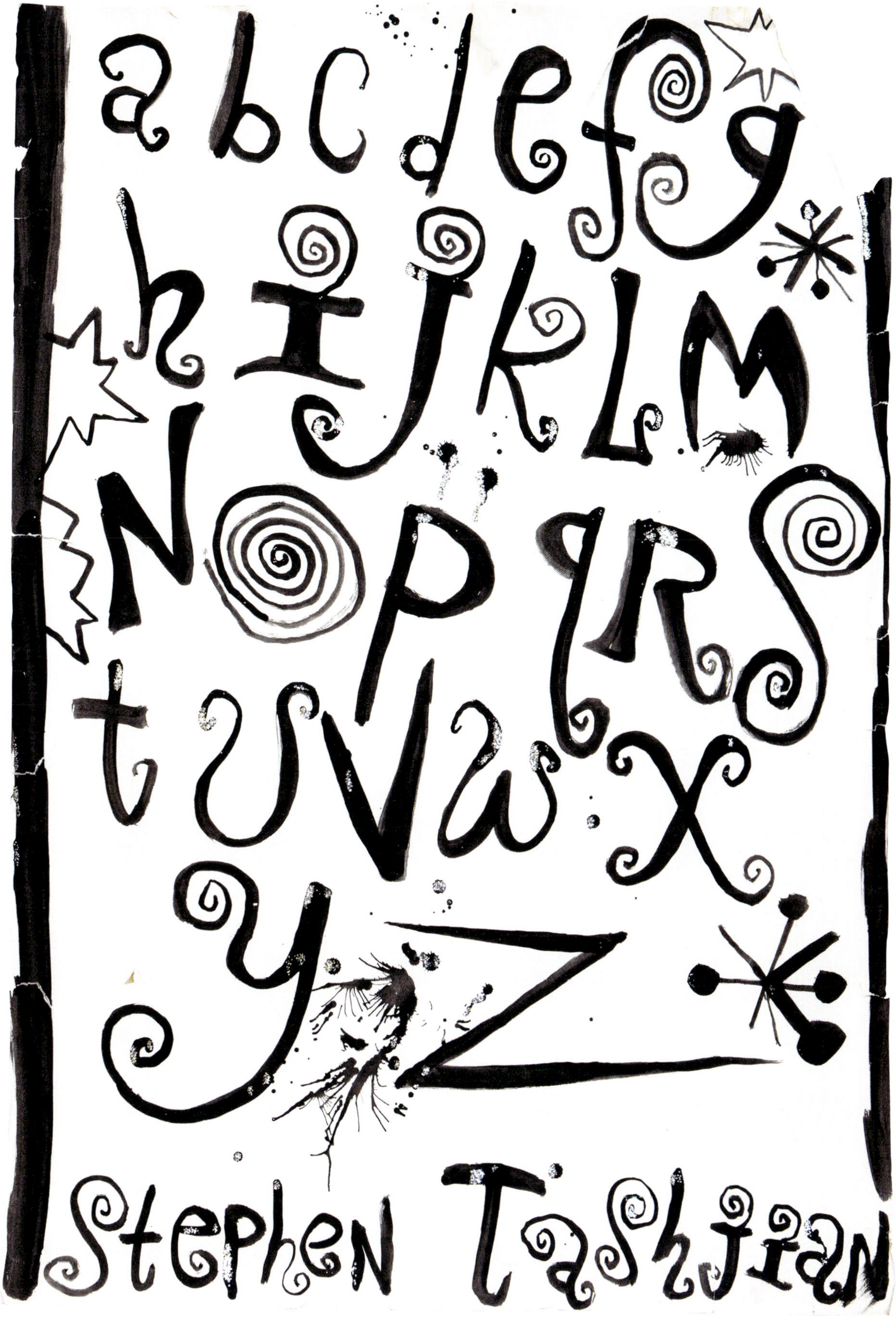

a b c d e f g
h i j k l m
n o p q r s
t u v w x
y z

Stephen Tashjian

Flamenco, 1988
Acrylic and glitter on paper
30 × 23 inches (76.2 × 58.4 cm)

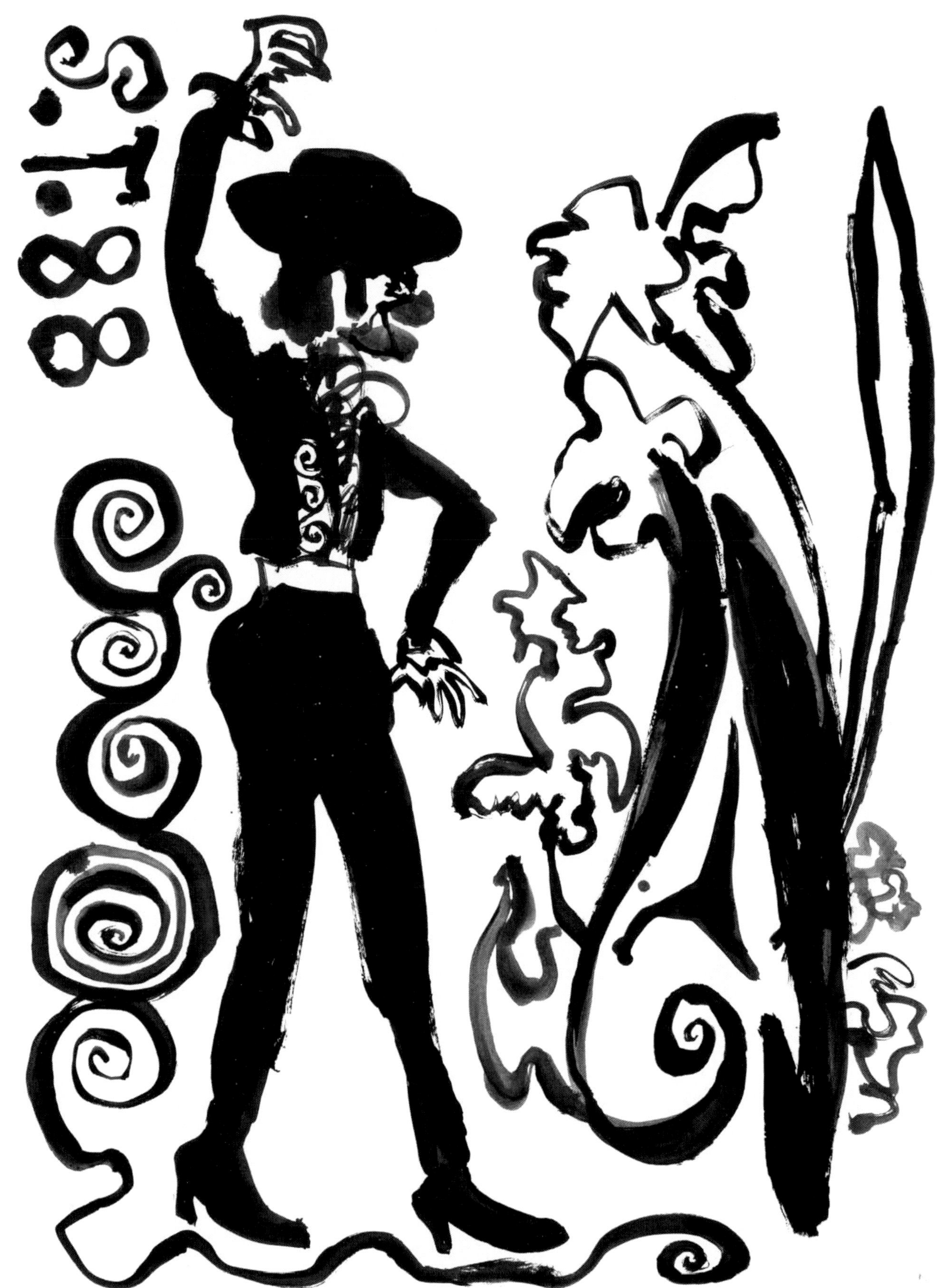

Your Pyramid, 1984
Acrylic and tape collage on paper
13 × 12½ inches (33 × 31.8 cm)

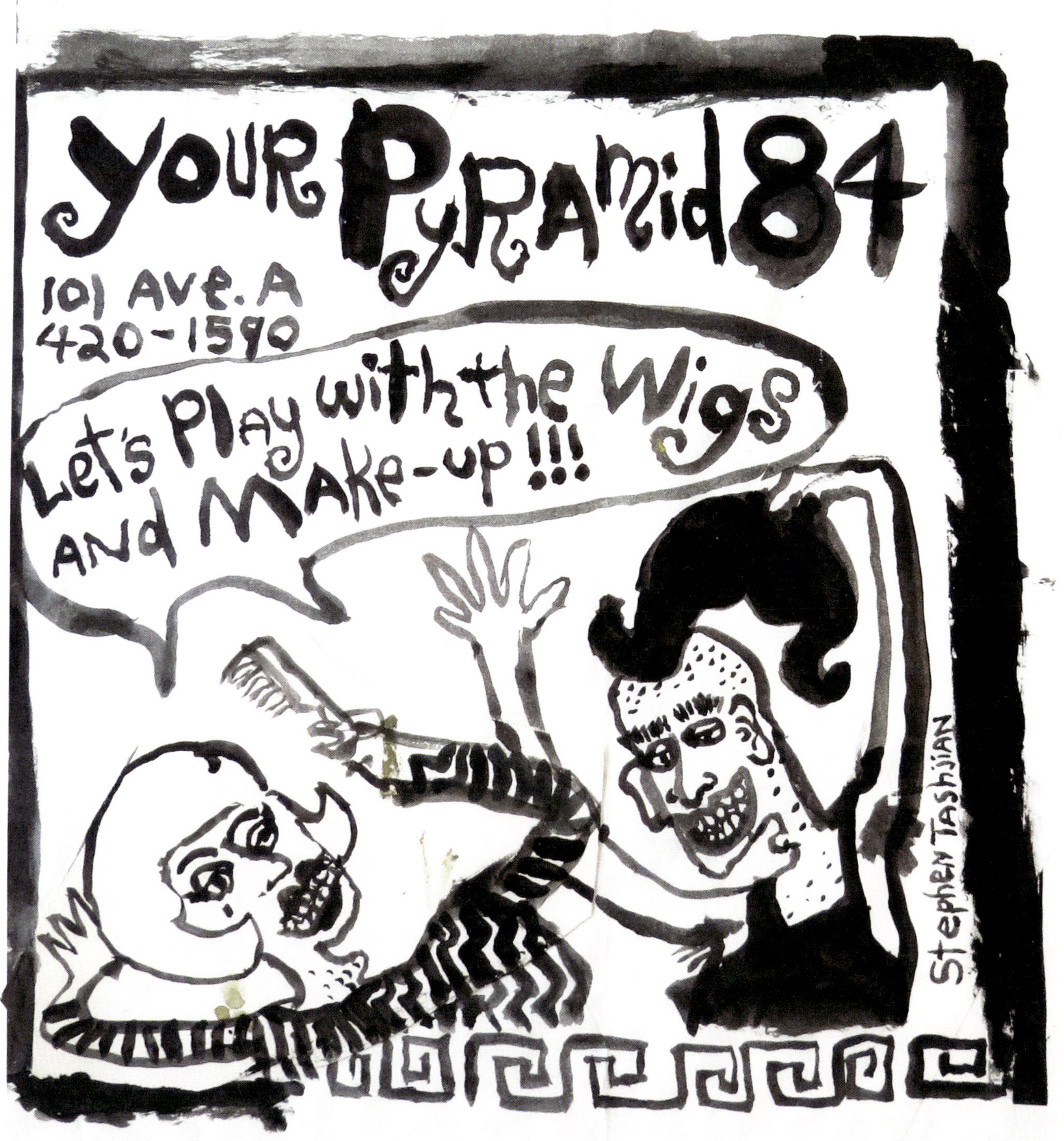

YOUR PyRAmid 84
101 AVE. A
420-1590
Let's Play with the Wigs and Make-up !!!
Stephen Tashjian

Your Pyramid, 1984
Acrylic, marker, tape, and collage on paper
13 × 12½ inches (33 × 31.8 cm)

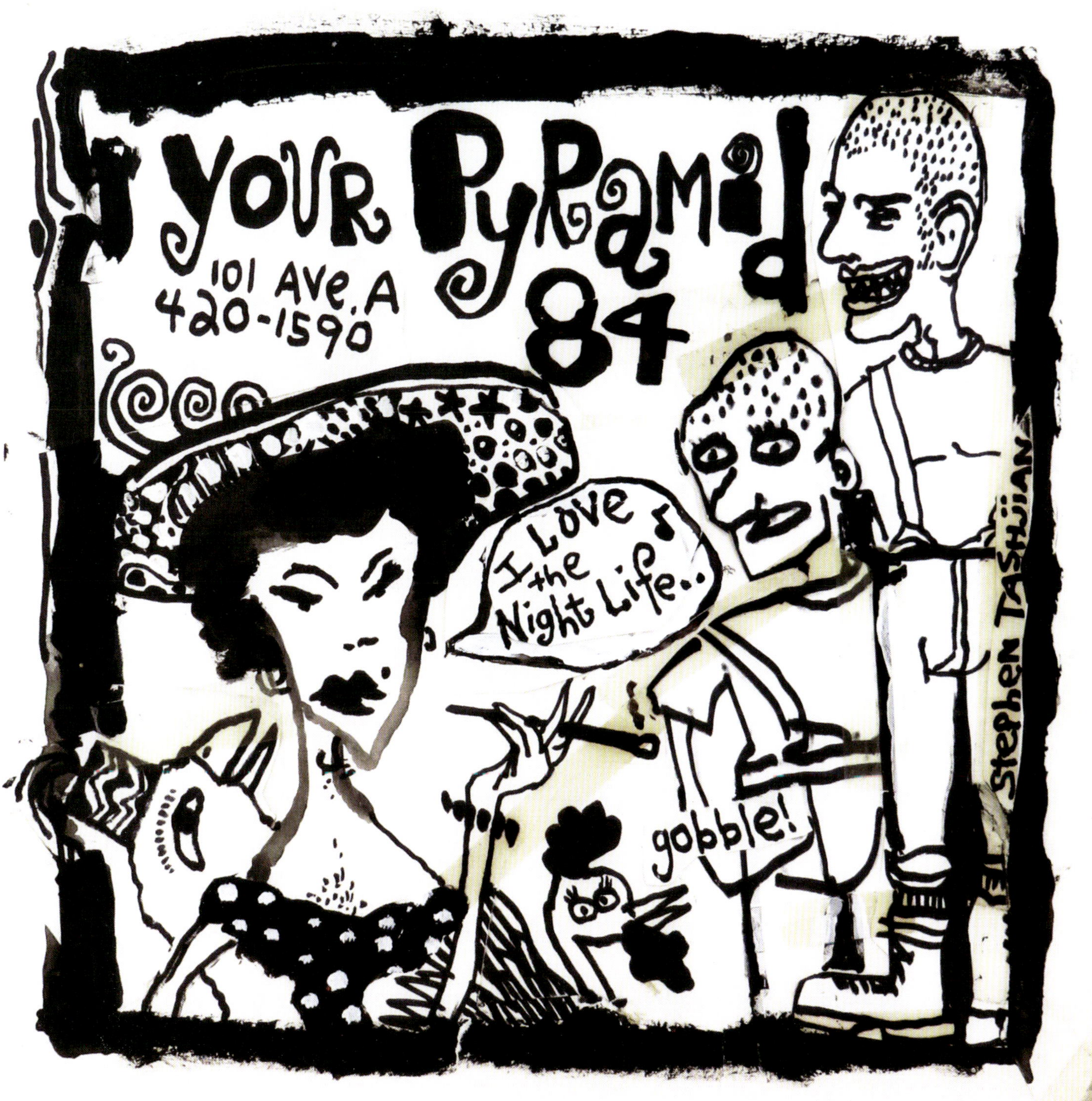
YOUR PYRAMID 84
101 AVE. A
420-1590
I LOVE the Night Life..
gobble!
STEPHEN TASHJIAN

Wonderful Colorful Pyramid, 1985
Acrylic and mixed-media collage on paper
18½ × 15 inches (47 × 38.1 cm)

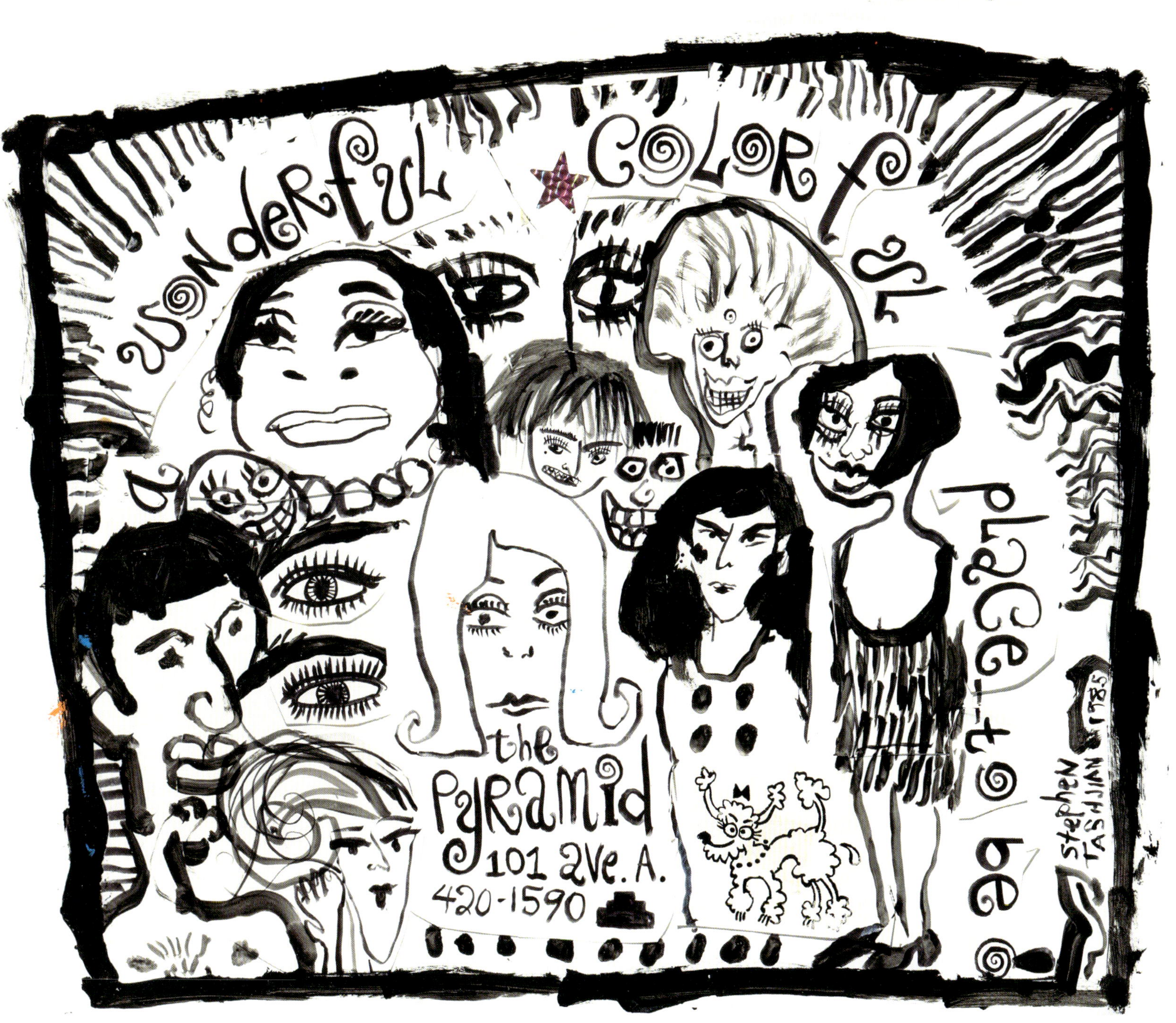
a wonderful COLORful place to be!
the Pyramid
101 ave. A.
420-1590
Stephen Tashjian 1985

EPHEMERA

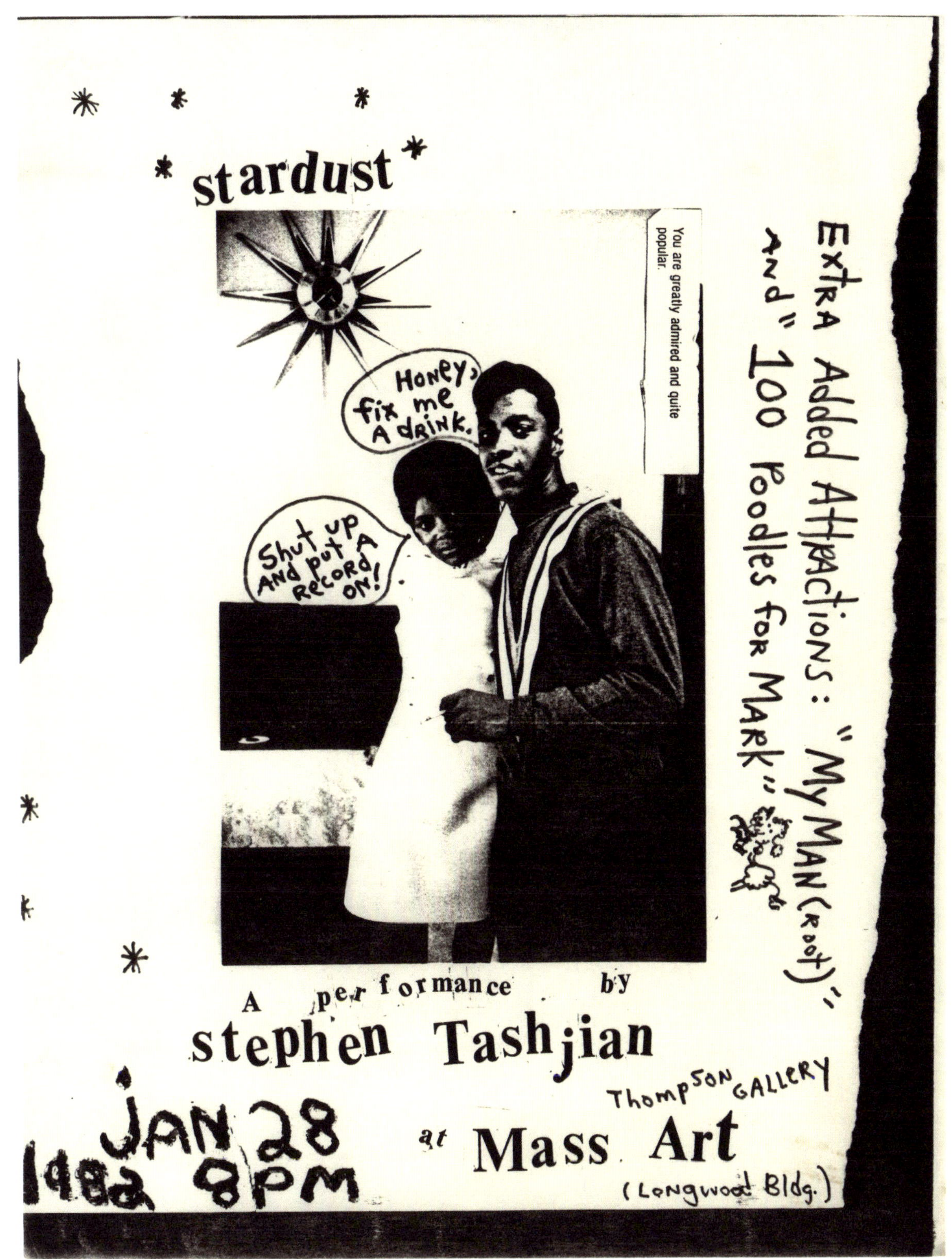

Stardust flyer, 1982, black-and-white photocopy, 11 × 8½ inches (27.9 × 21.6 cm)

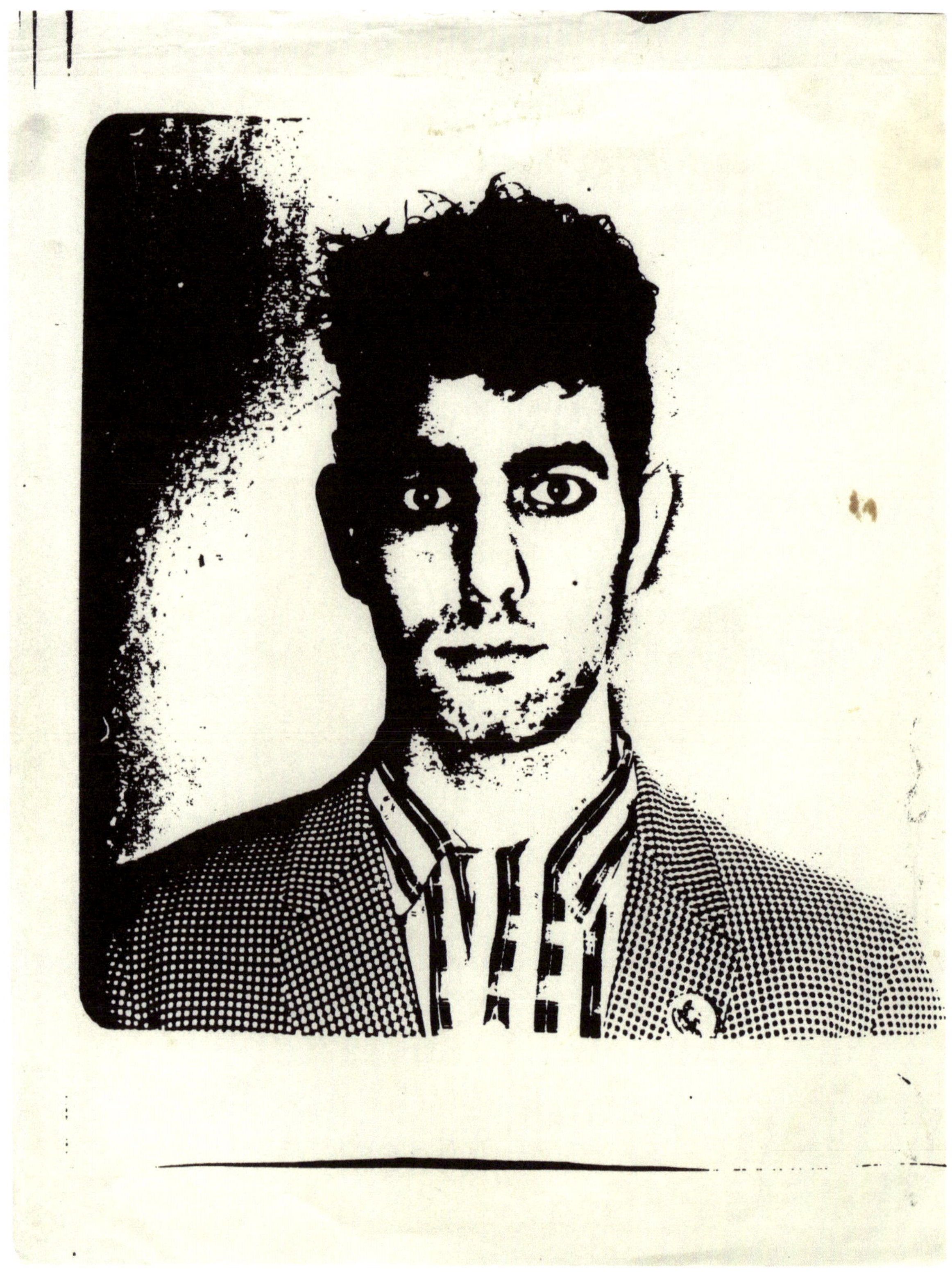

Untitled (Self-Portrait), 1980s, black-and-white photocopy, 11 × 8½ inches (27.9 × 21.6 cm)

Lucky Strike flyer, 1982, black-and-white photocopy, 6½ × 4½ inches (16.5 × 11.4 cm)

Tabboo! and Mark Rizzo, Philly's Piercing of Jimmy Paulette Flyer, 1980s,
black-and-white photocopy, 11 × 8½ inches (27.9 × 21.6 cm)

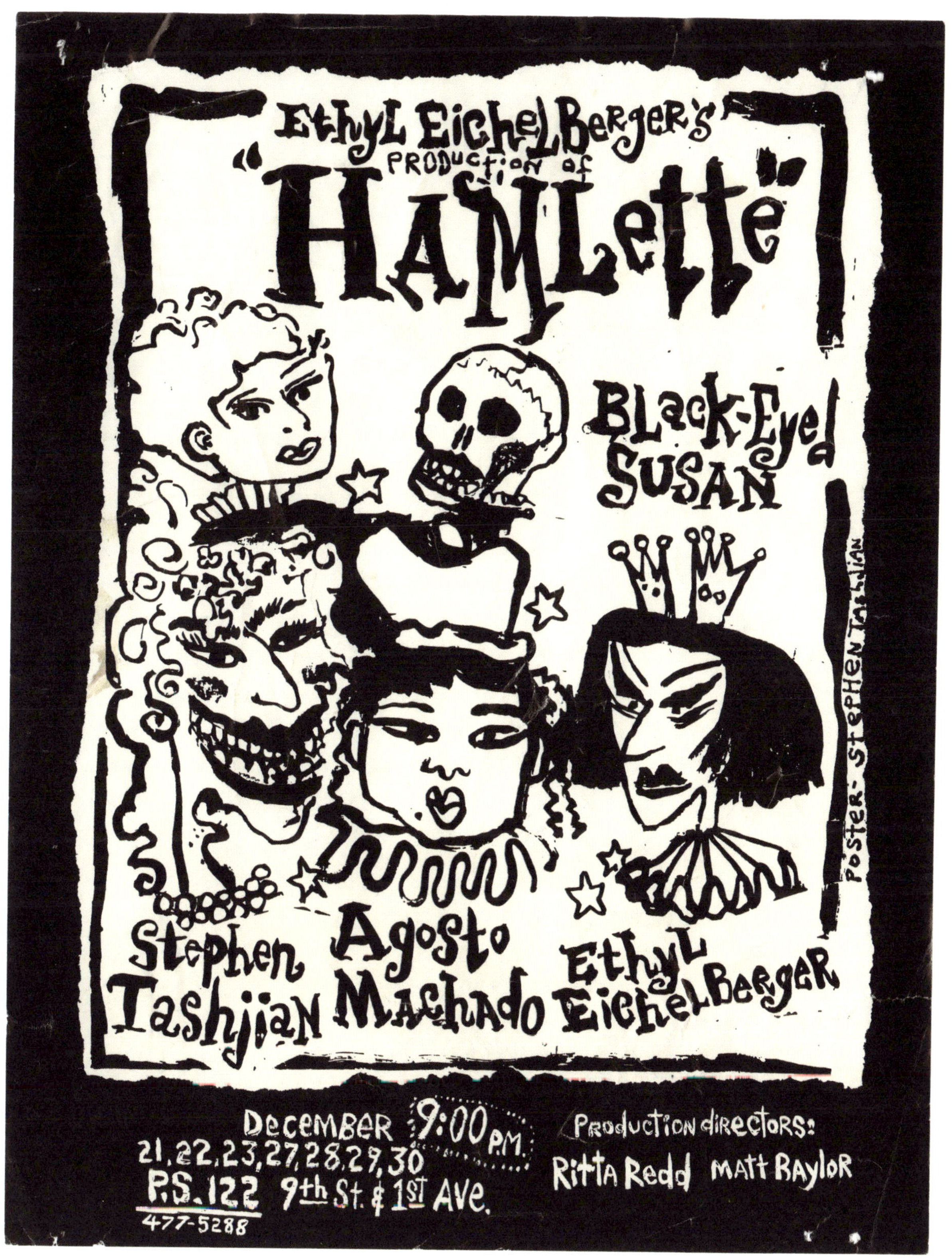

Ethyl Eichelberger's Hamlette flyer, ca. 1985, black-and-white photocopy, 11 × 8½ inches (27.9 × 21.6 cm)

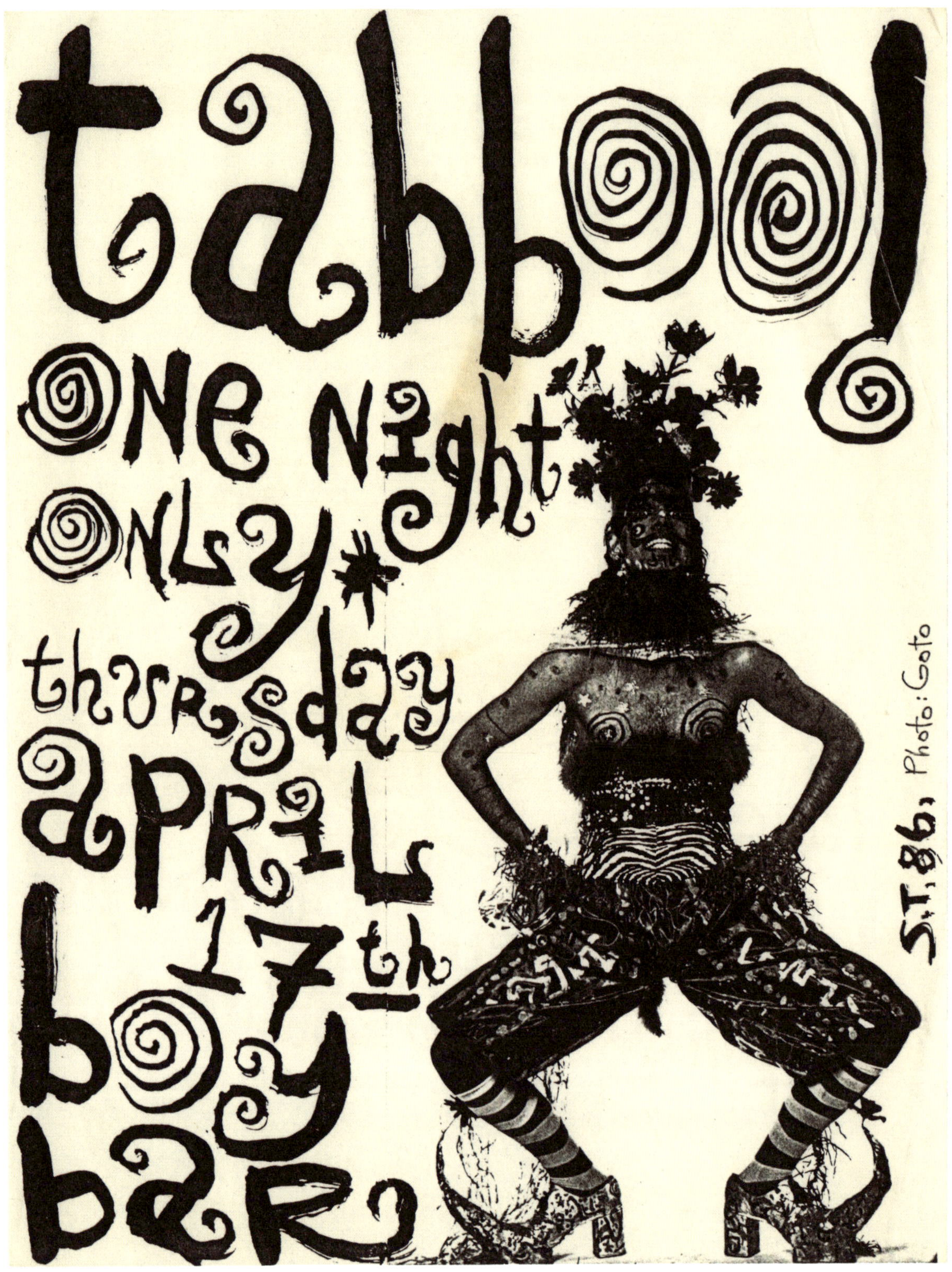

Boy Bar flyer, 1986, black-and-white photocopy, 11 × 8½ inches (27.9 × 21.6 cm)

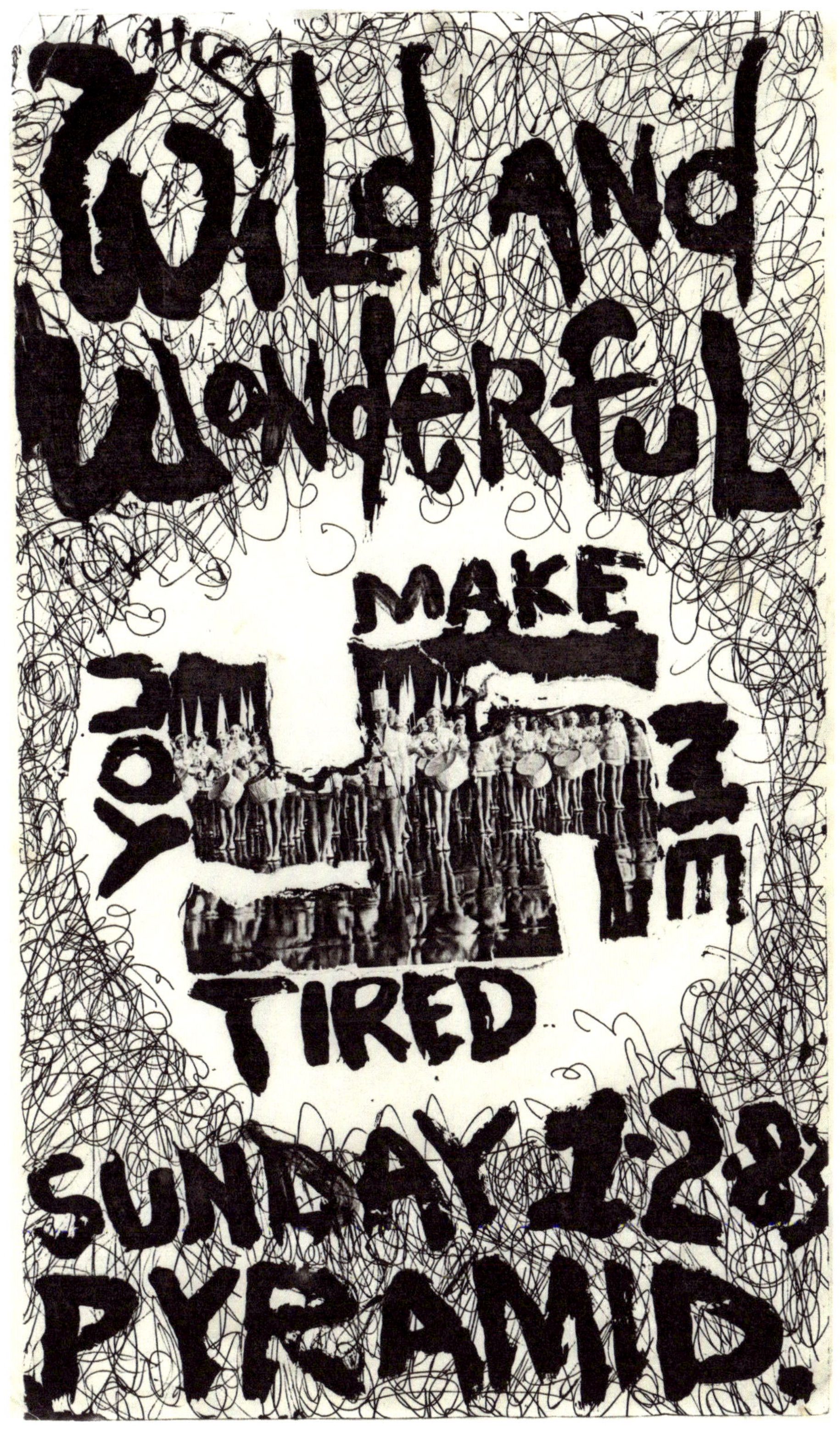

Wild and Wonderful flyer, 1983, black-and-white photocopy, 14 × 8½ inches (35.6 × 21.6 cm)

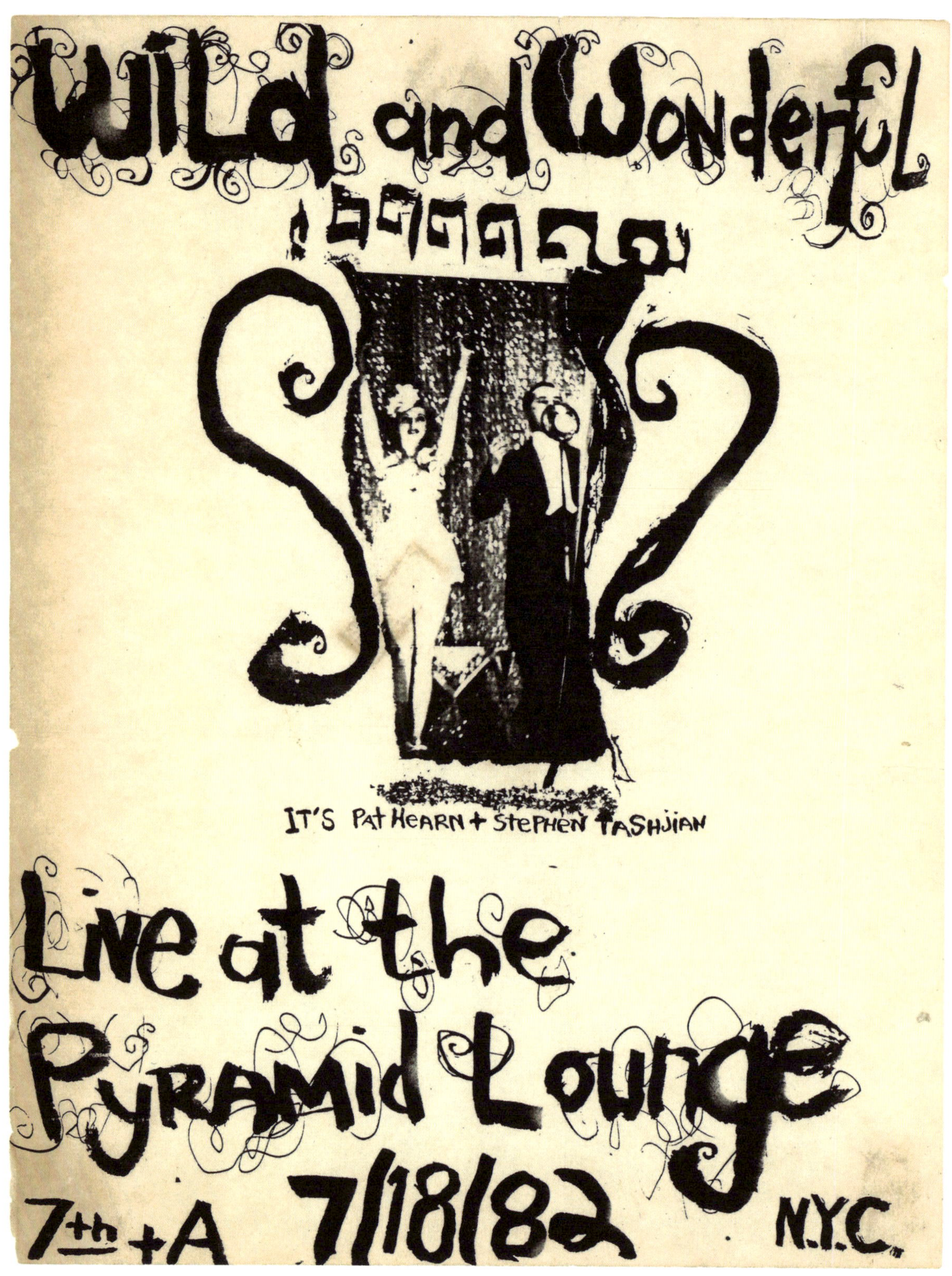

Wild and Wonderful flyer, 1986, black-and-white photocopy, 11 × 8½ inches (27.9 × 21.6 cm)

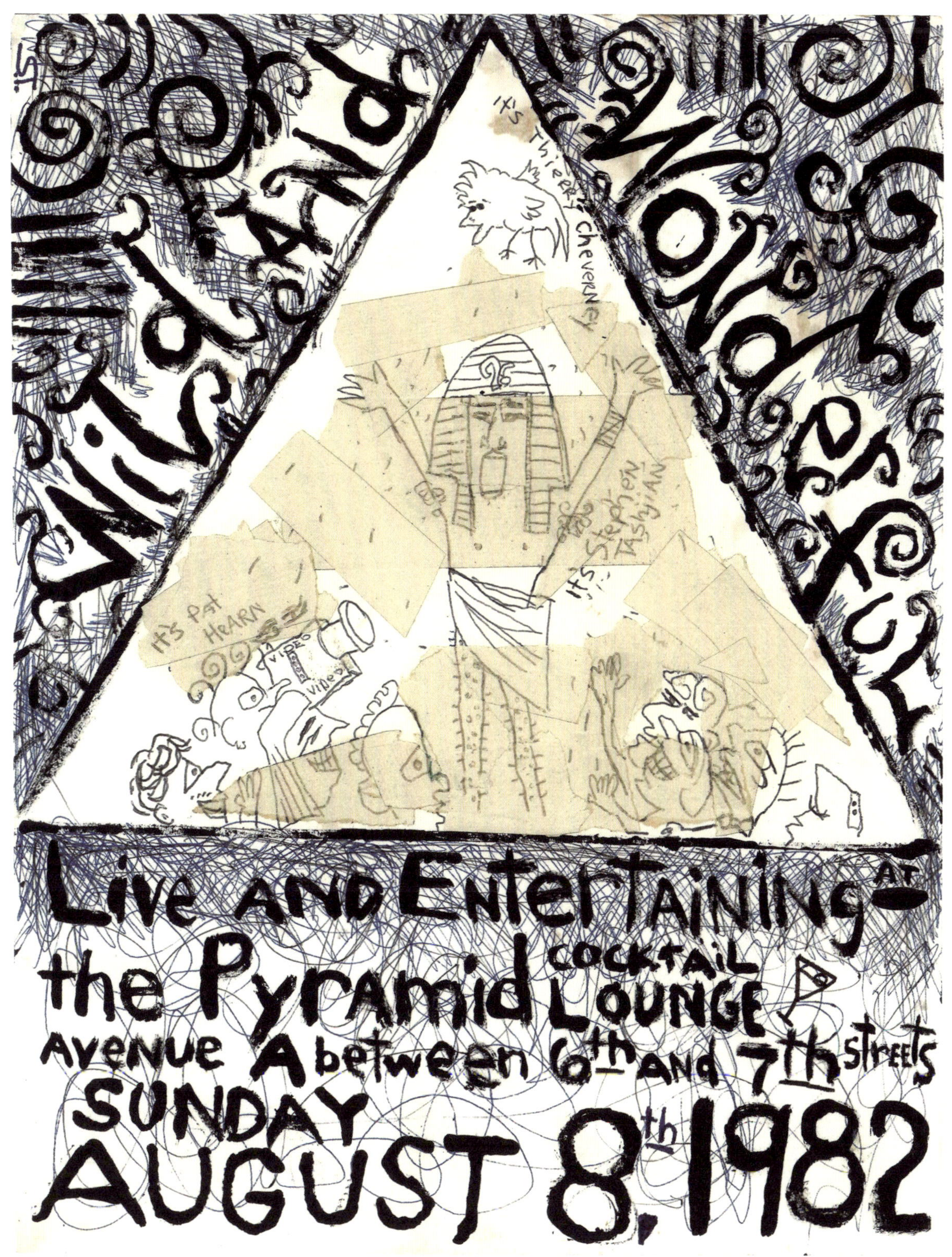

Wild and Wonderful flyer, 1982, acrylic, pen, and tape on paper, 11 × 8½ inches (27.9 × 21.6 cm)

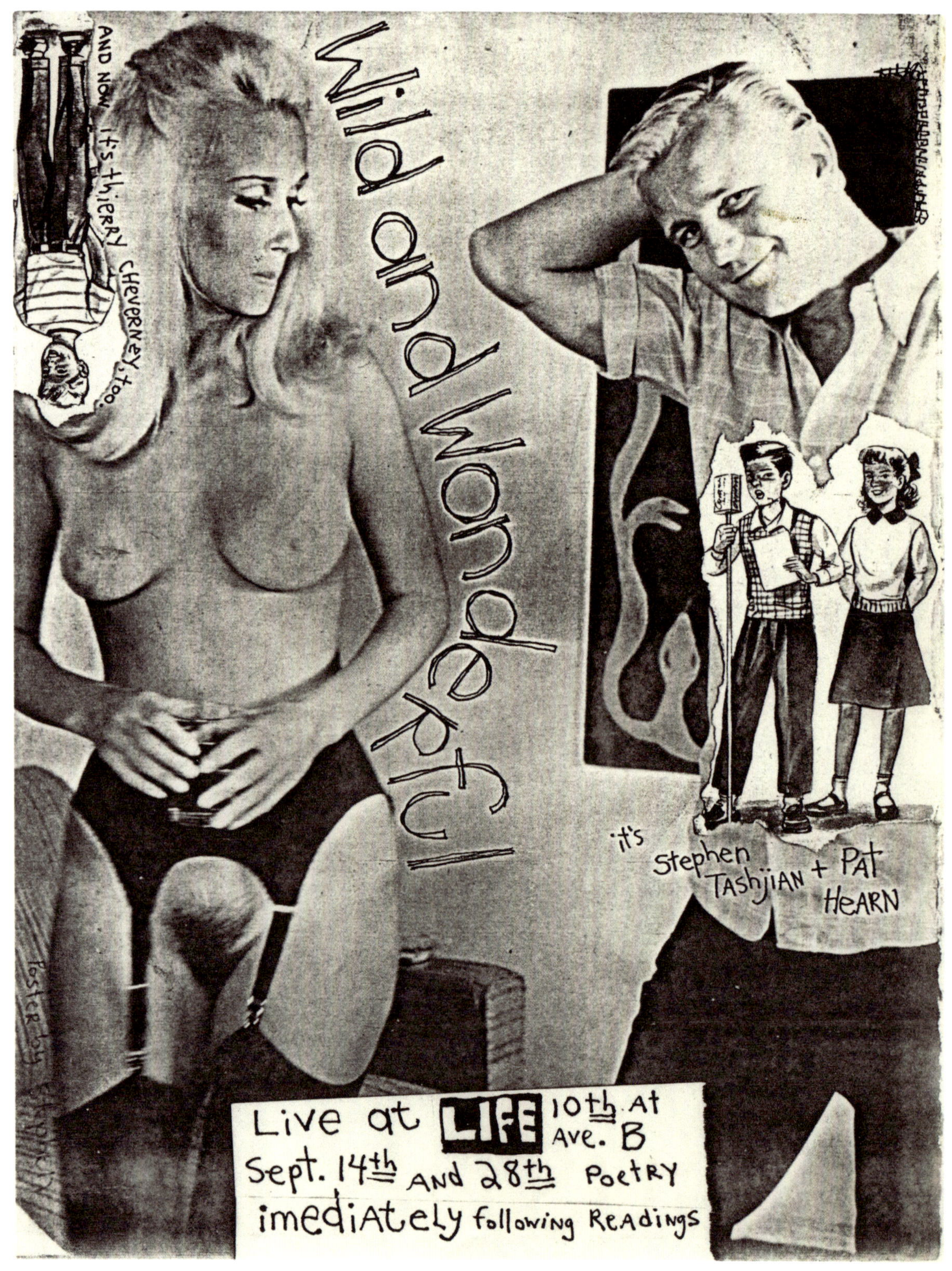

Wild and Wonderful flyer, 1982, black-and-white photocopy, 11 × 8½ inches (27.9 × 21.6 cm)

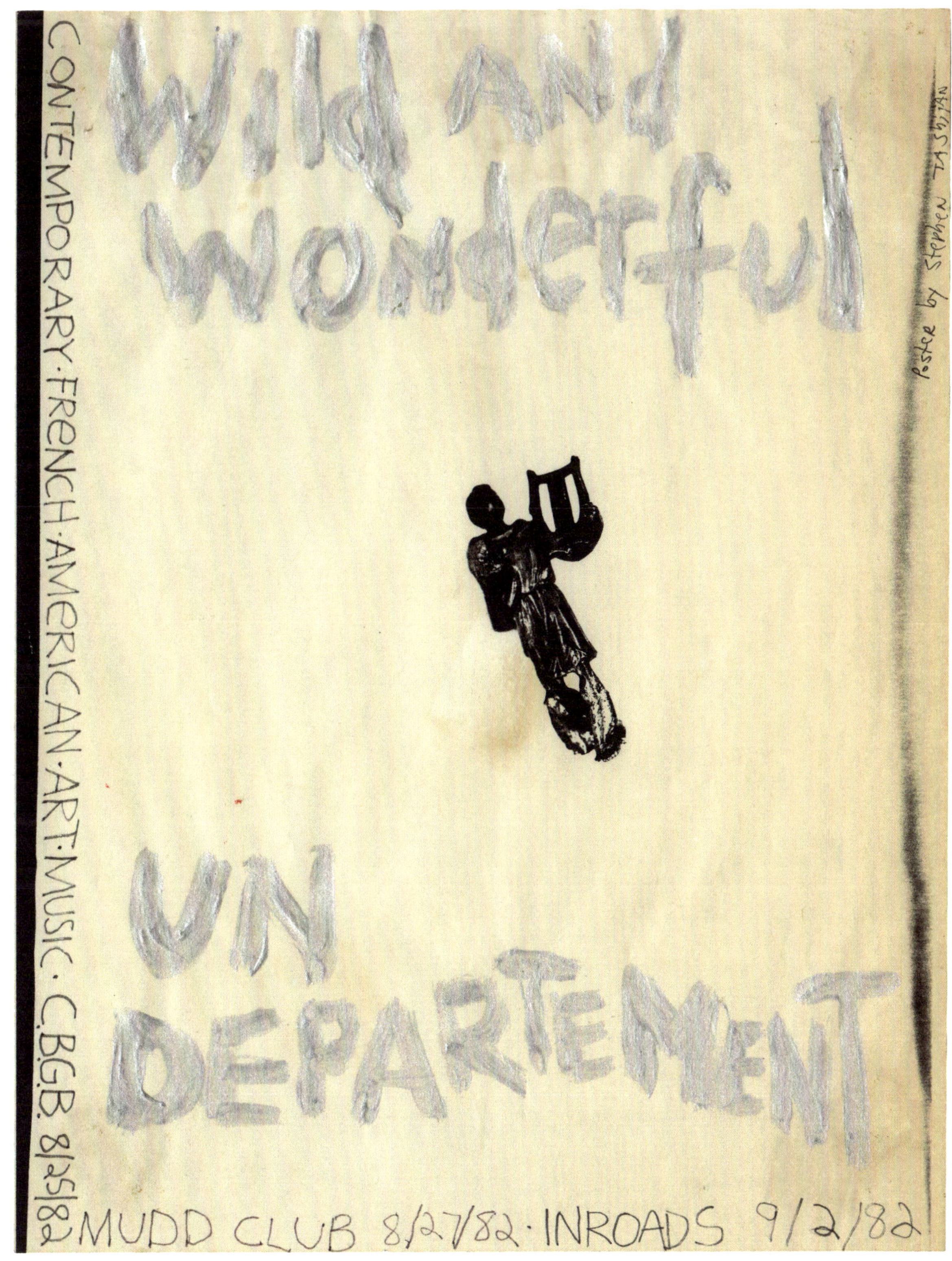

Wild and Wonderful flyer, 1982, black-and-white photocopy, acrylic, and pen on paper, 11 × 8½ inches (27.9 × 21.6 cm)

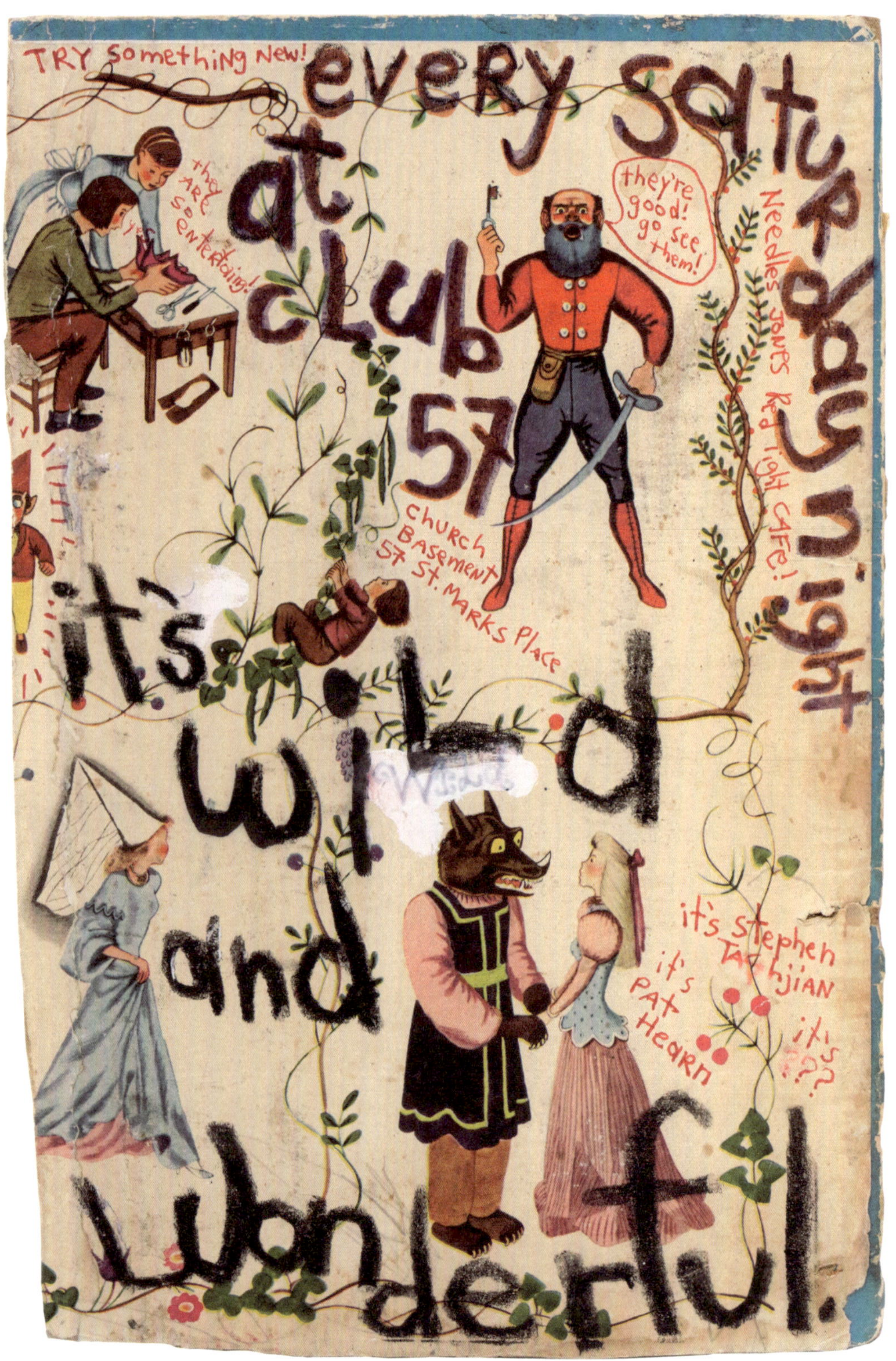

Wild and Wonderful, n.d., ink and crayon on paper board, 10¾ × 7¼ inches (27.3 × 18.4 cm)

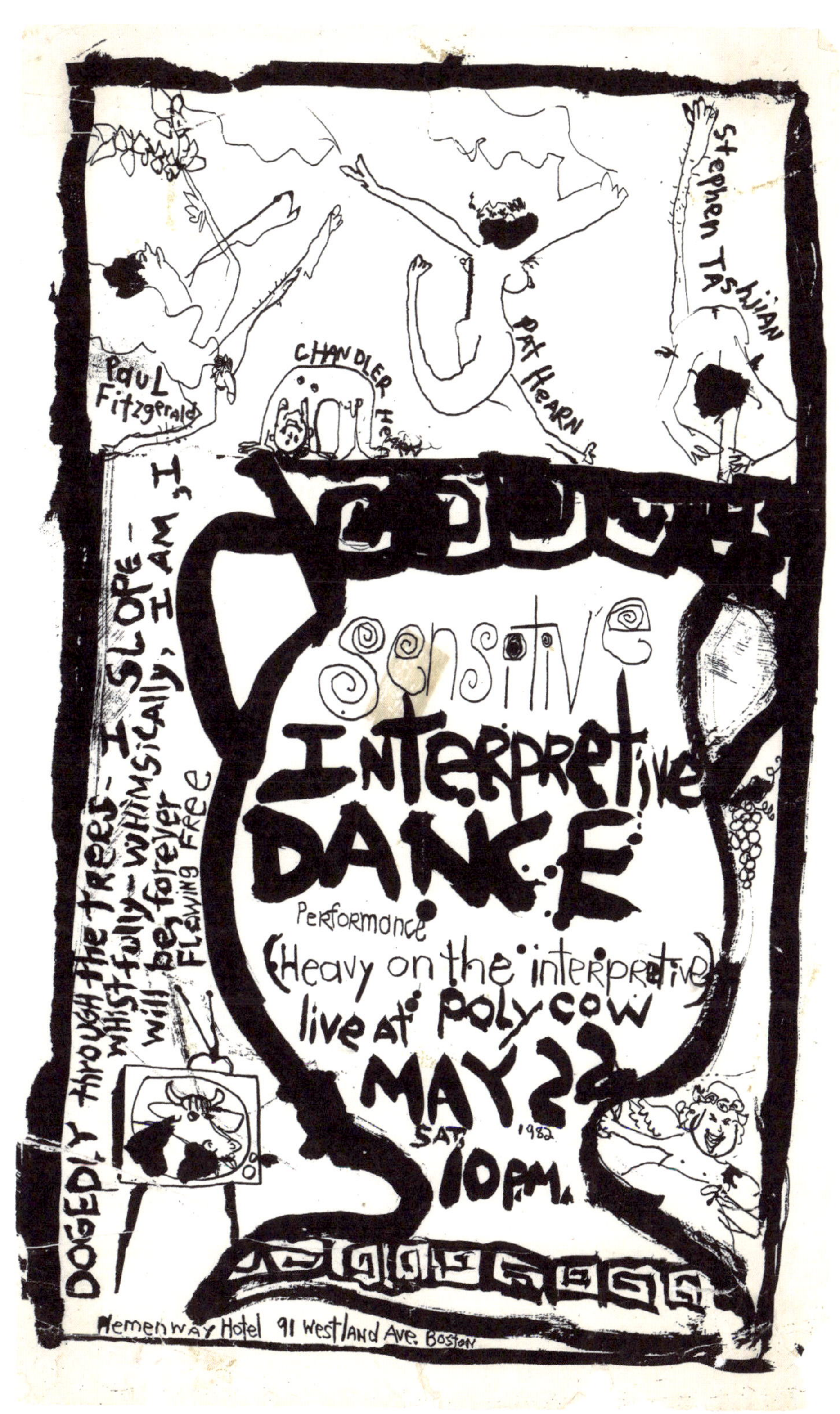

Sensitive Interpretive Dance flyer, 1982, black-and-white photocopy, 14 × 8½ inches (35.6 × 21.6 cm)

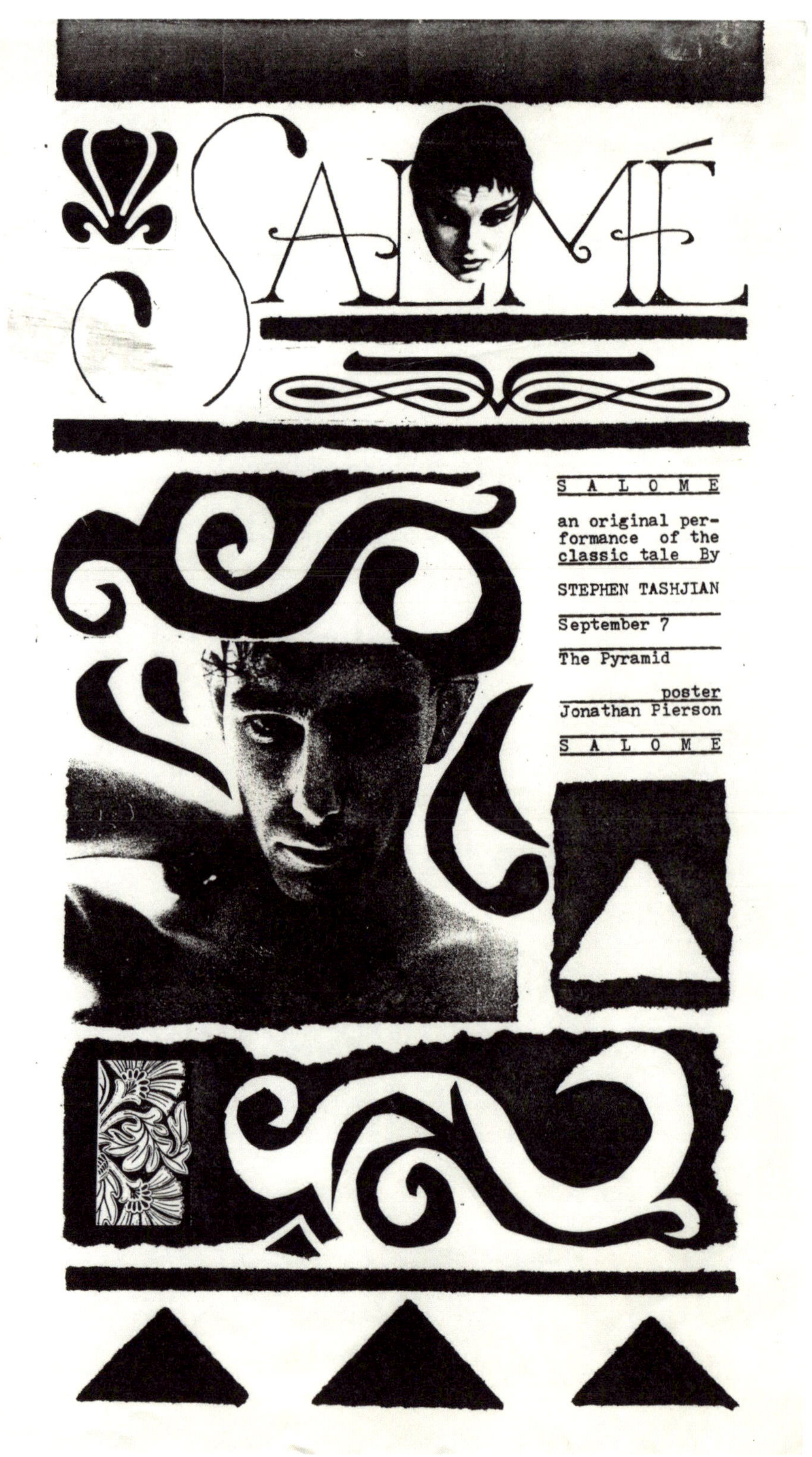

Jack Pierson, Tabboo!'s Salomé flyer, 1980s, black-and-white photocopy, 14 × 8½ inches (35.6 × 21.6 cm)

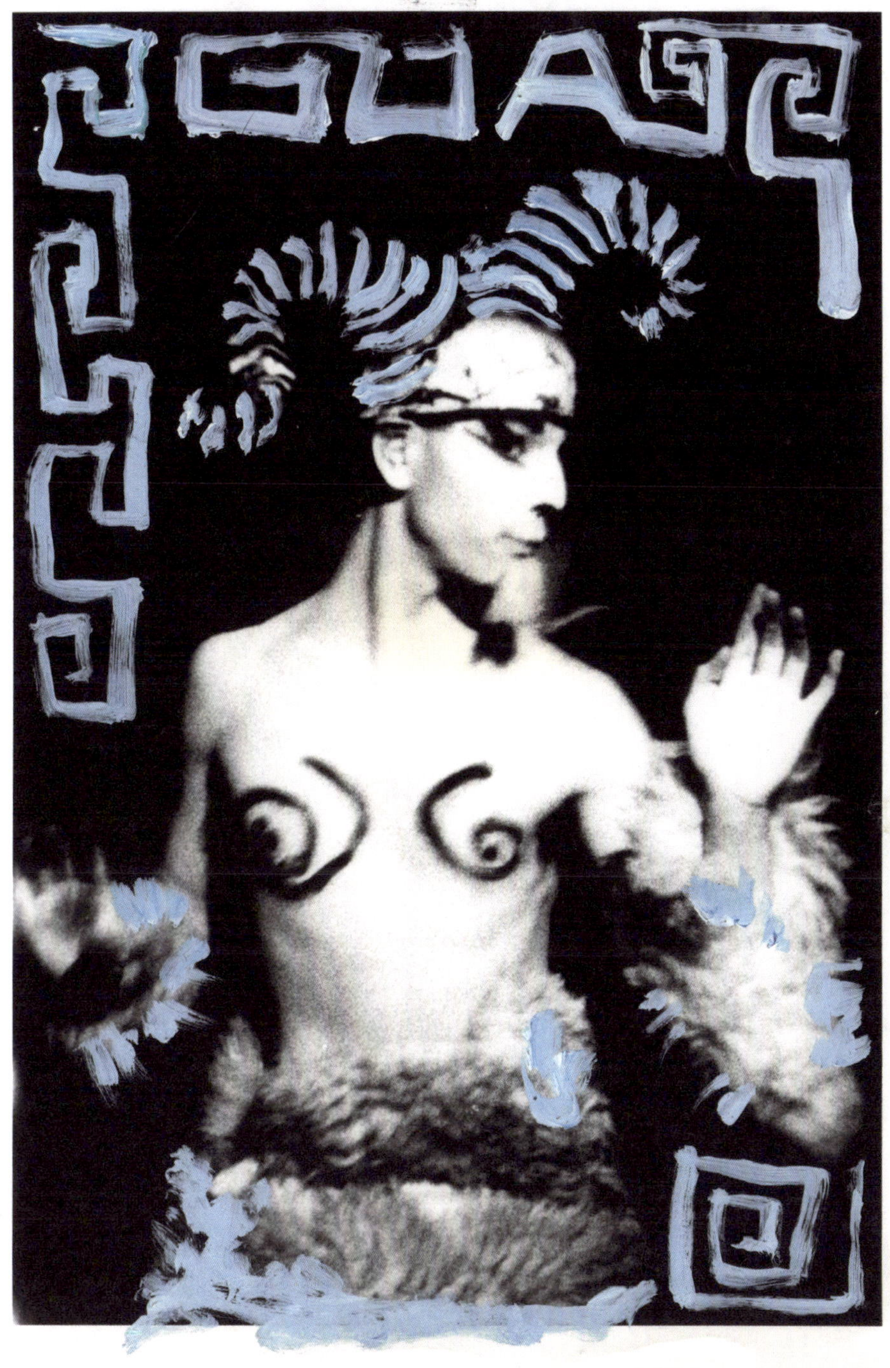

Unknown photographer, Tabboo! performing in his goat costume with papier-mâché horns, ca. 1984, acrylic on silver gelatin print, 14 × 11 inches (35.6 × 27.9 cm)

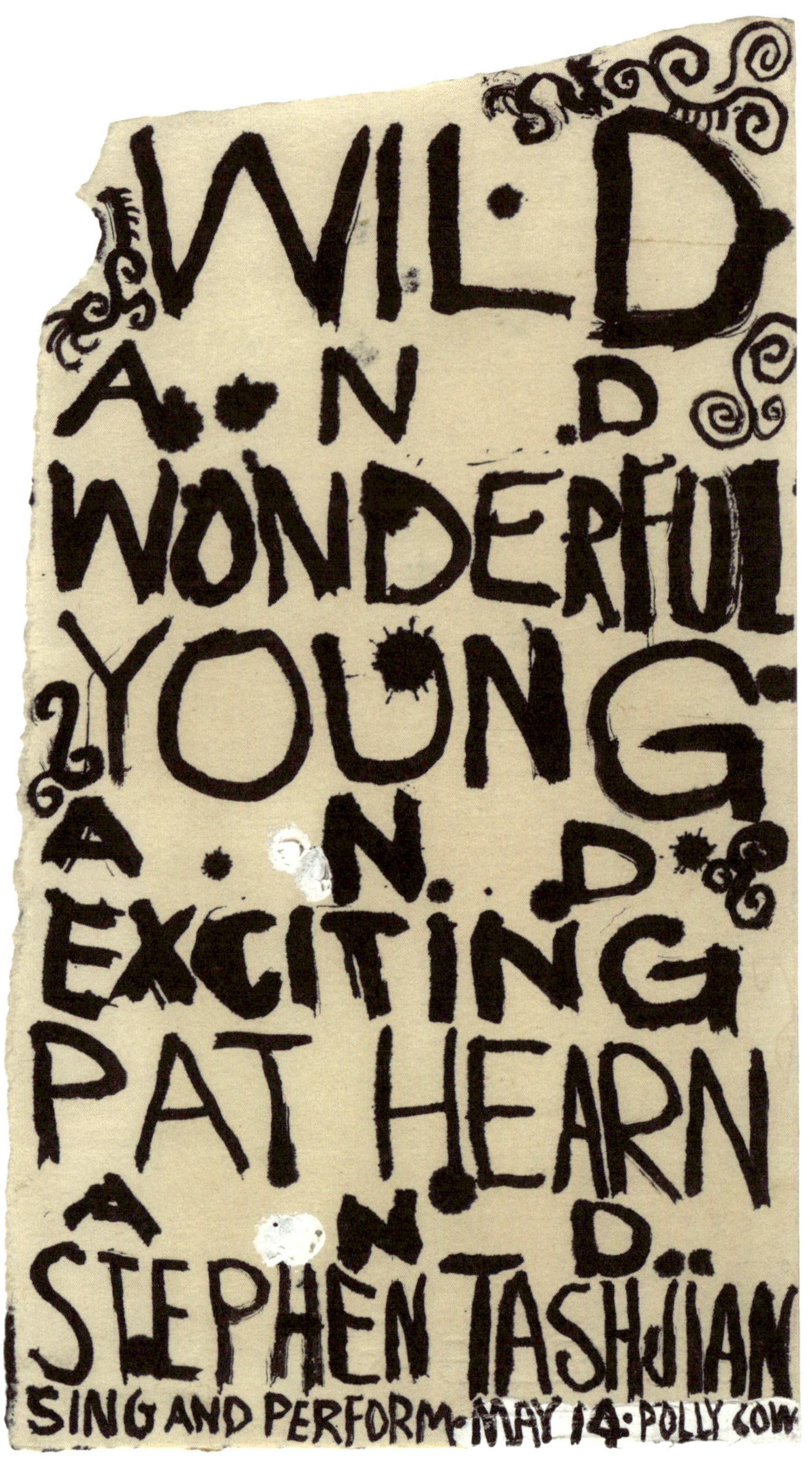

Drawing for Wild and Wonderful flyer, ca. 1982, acrylic on paper, 12 × 7 inches (30.5 × 17.8 cm)

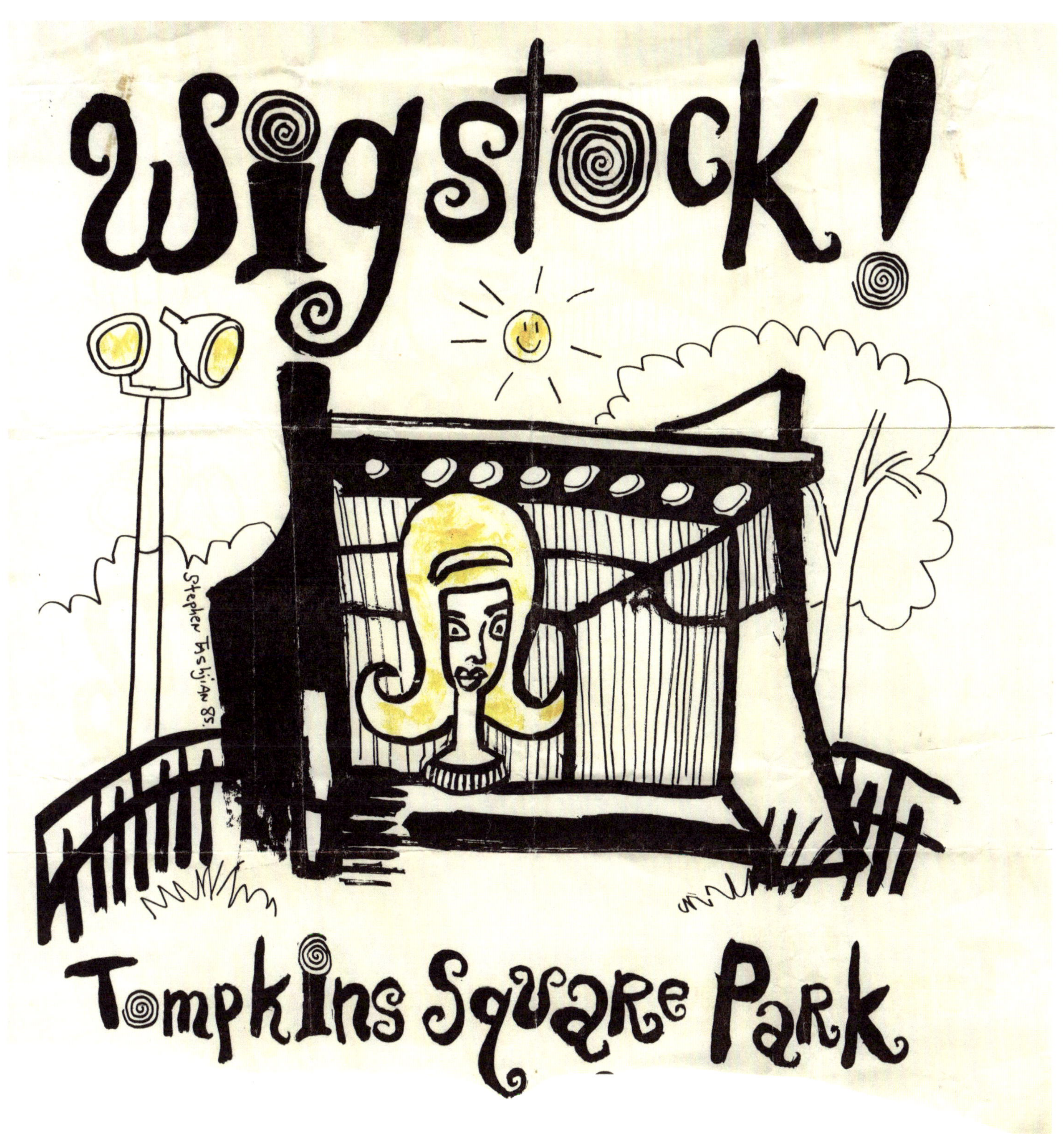

Wigstock poster, 1984, acrylic, marker, tape, and collage on paper, 13 × 12½ inches (33 × 31.8 cm)

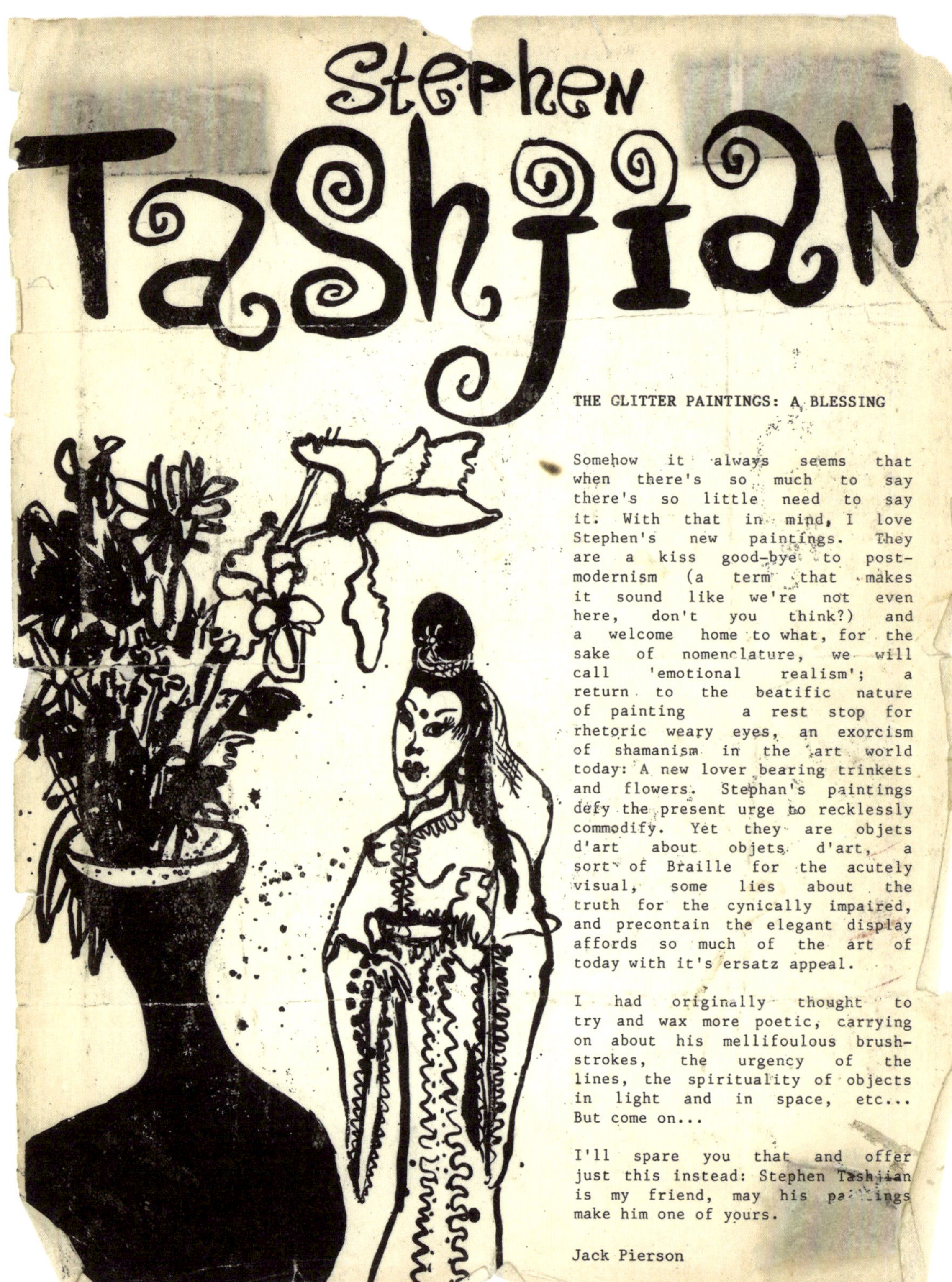

Stephen
Tashjian

THE GLITTER PAINTINGS: A BLESSING

Somehow it always seems that when there's so much to say there's so little need to say it. With that in mind, I love Stephen's new paintings. They are a kiss good-bye to post-modernism (a term that makes it sound like we're not even here, don't you think?) and a welcome home to what, for the sake of nomenclature, we will call 'emotional realism'; a return to the beatific nature of painting a rest stop for rhetoric weary eyes, an exorcism of shamanism in the art world today: A new lover bearing trinkets and flowers. Stephan's paintings defy the present urge to recklessly commodify. Yet they are objets d'art about objets d'art, a sort of Braille for the acutely visual, some lies about the truth for the cynically impaired, and precontain the elegant display affords so much of the art of today with it's ersatz appeal.

I had originally thought to try and wax more poetic, carrying on about his mellifoulous brush-strokes, the urgency of the lines, the spirituality of objects in light and in space, etc... But come on...

I'll spare you that and offer just this instead: Stephen Tashjian is my friend, may his paintings make him one of yours.

Jack Pierson

Flyer for Stephen Tashjian, *The Glitter Paintings*, with text by Jack Pierson, 1986, black-and-white photocopy, 11 × 8½ inches (27.9 × 21.6 cm)

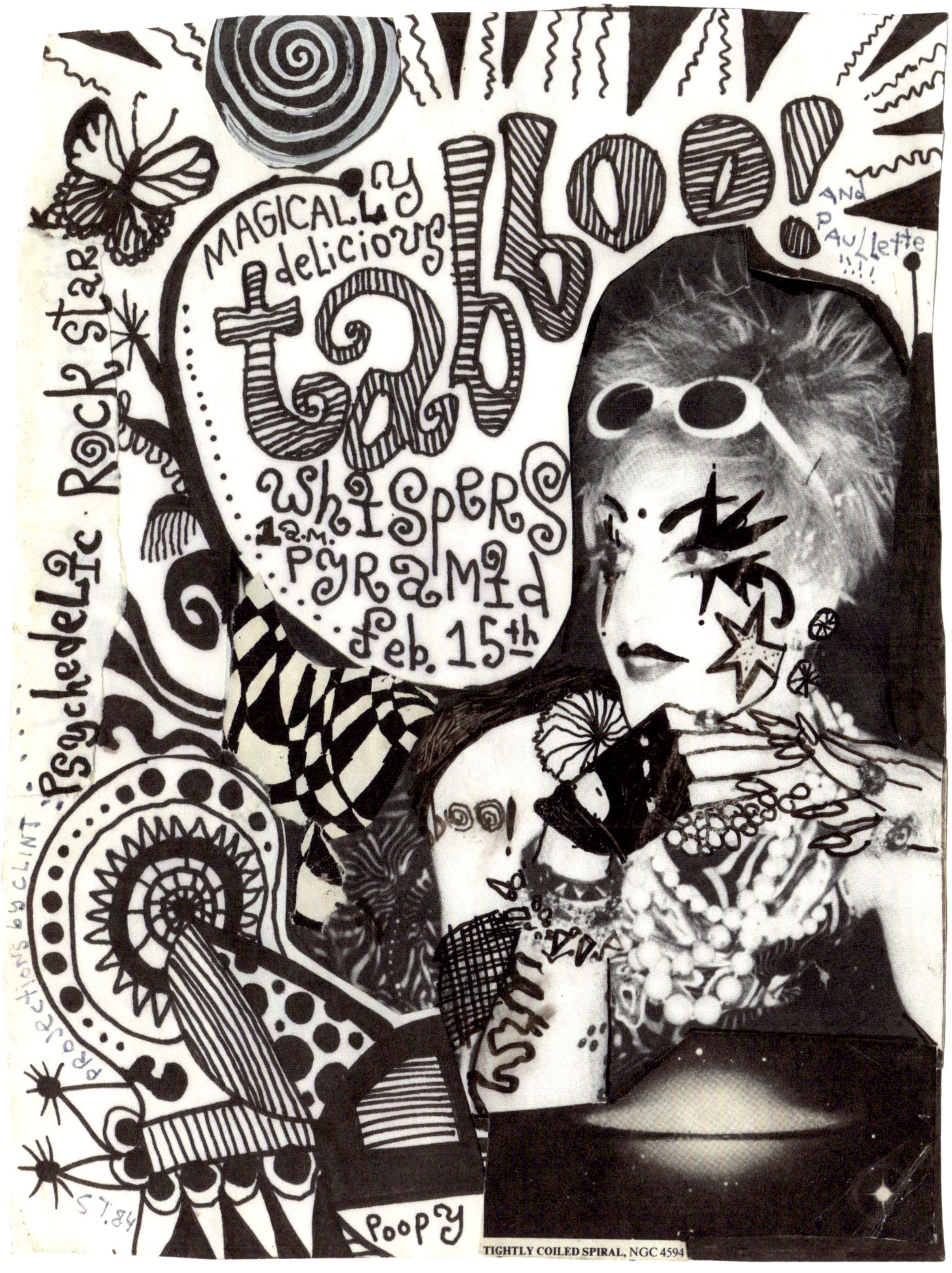

Drawing for Whispers flyer, 1984, acrylic, marker, pen, and collage on paper, 11 × 8½ inches (27.9 × 21.6 cm)

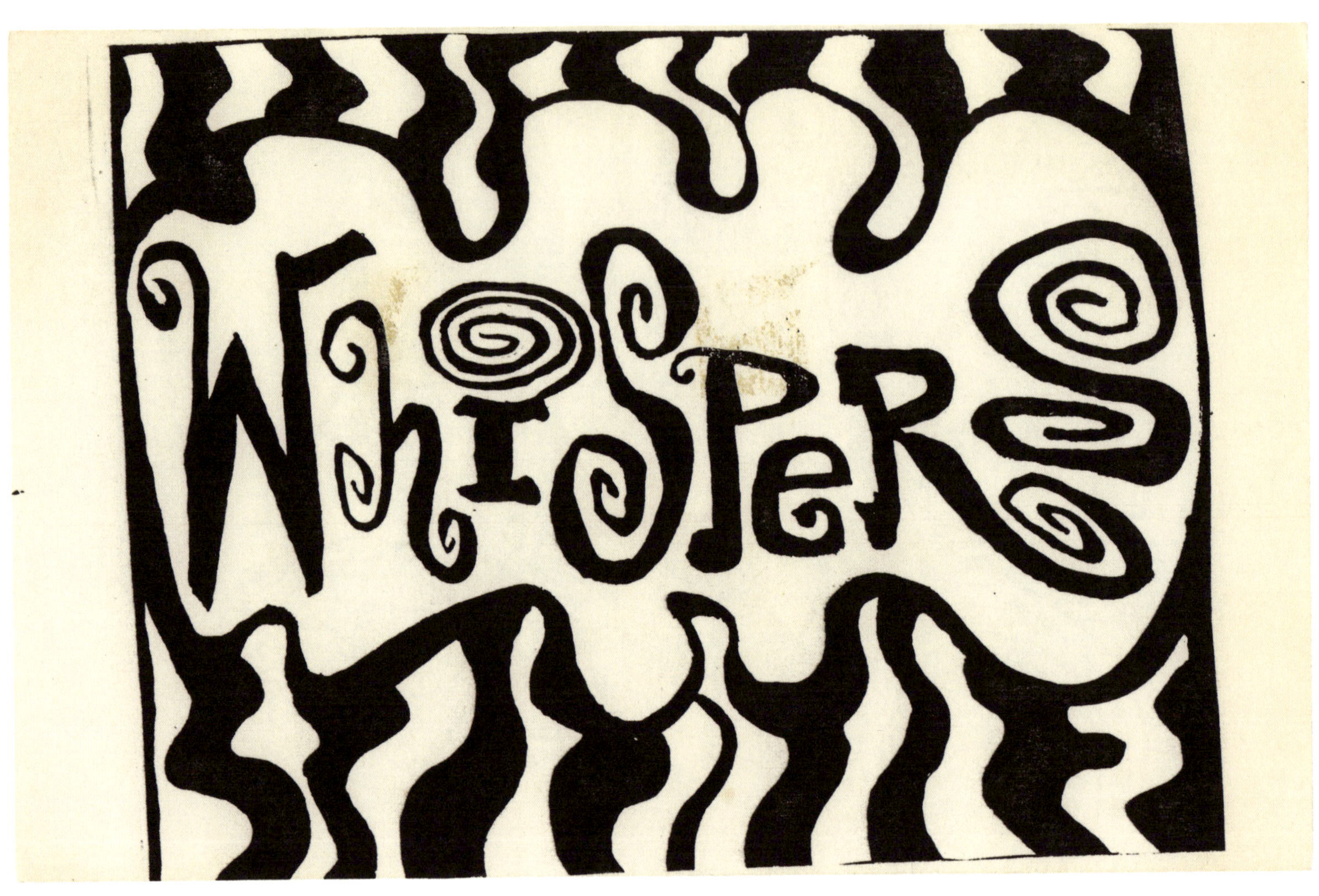

Whispers flyer, 1989, offset on paper, 5½ × 8½ inches (14 × 21.6 cm)

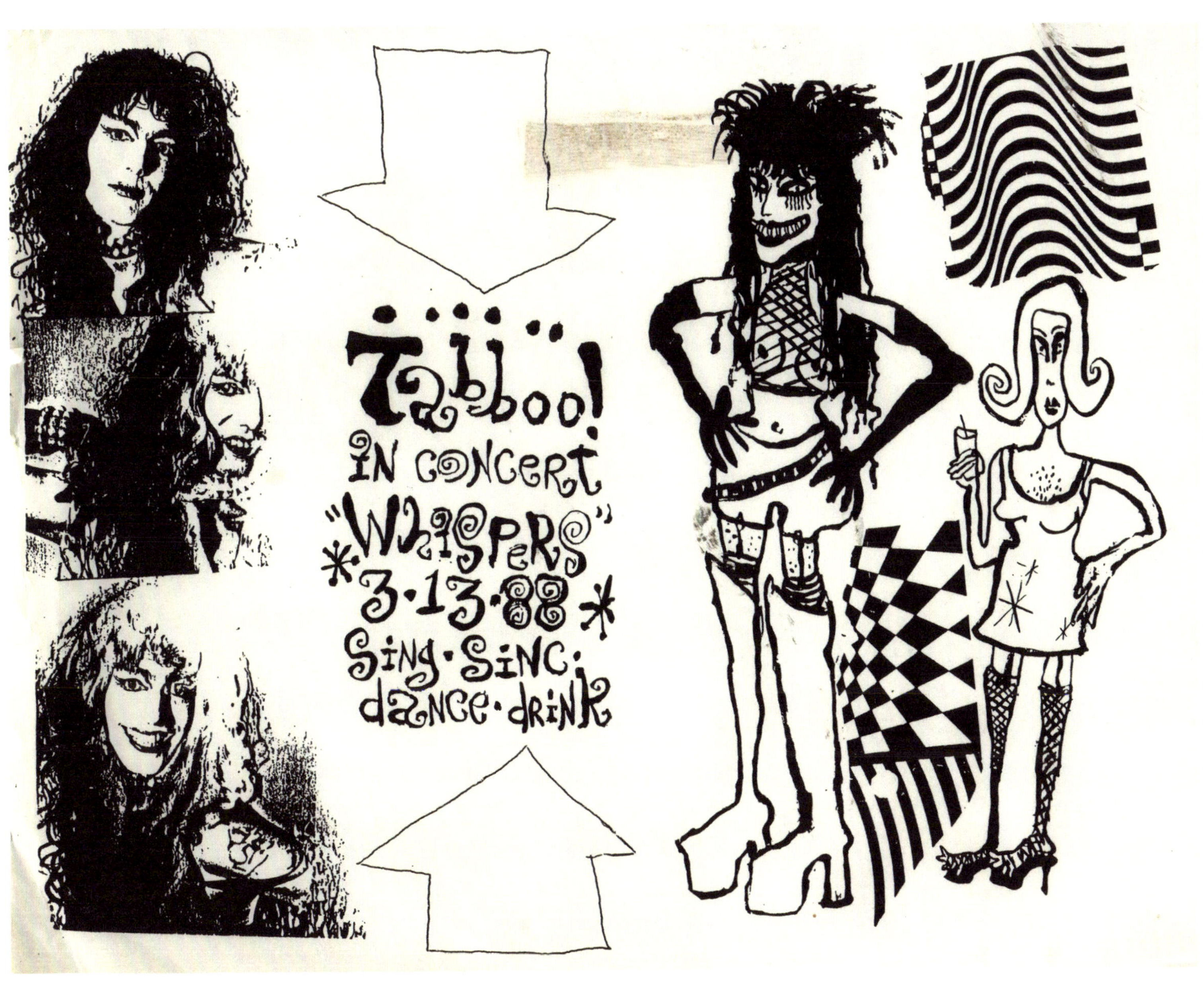

Whispers flyer, 1988, black-and-white photocopy, 8½ × 11 inches (21.6 × 27.9 cm)

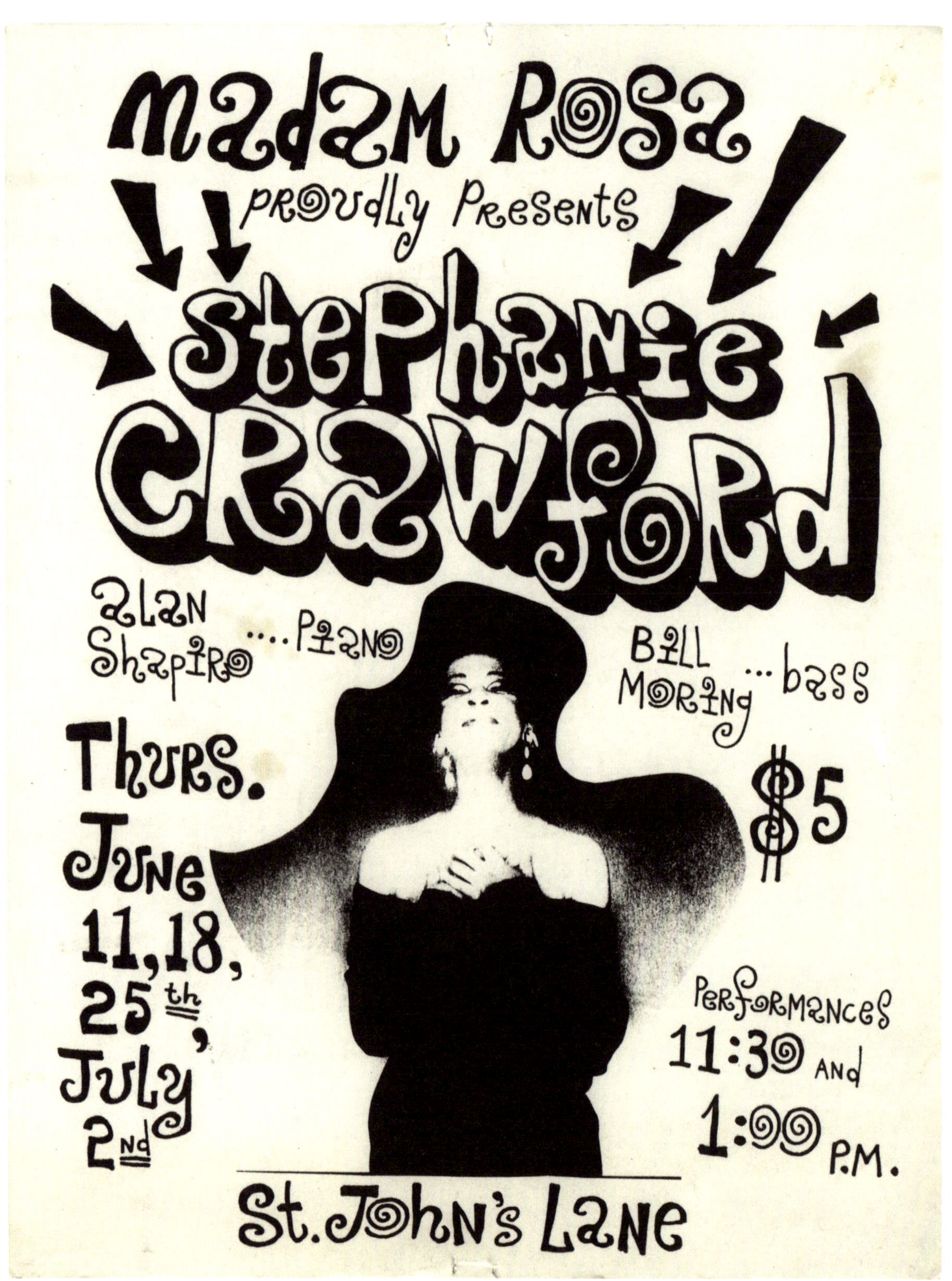

Stephanie Crawford flyer, ca. 1986, black-and-white photocopy, 11 × 8½ inches (27.9 × 21.6 cm)

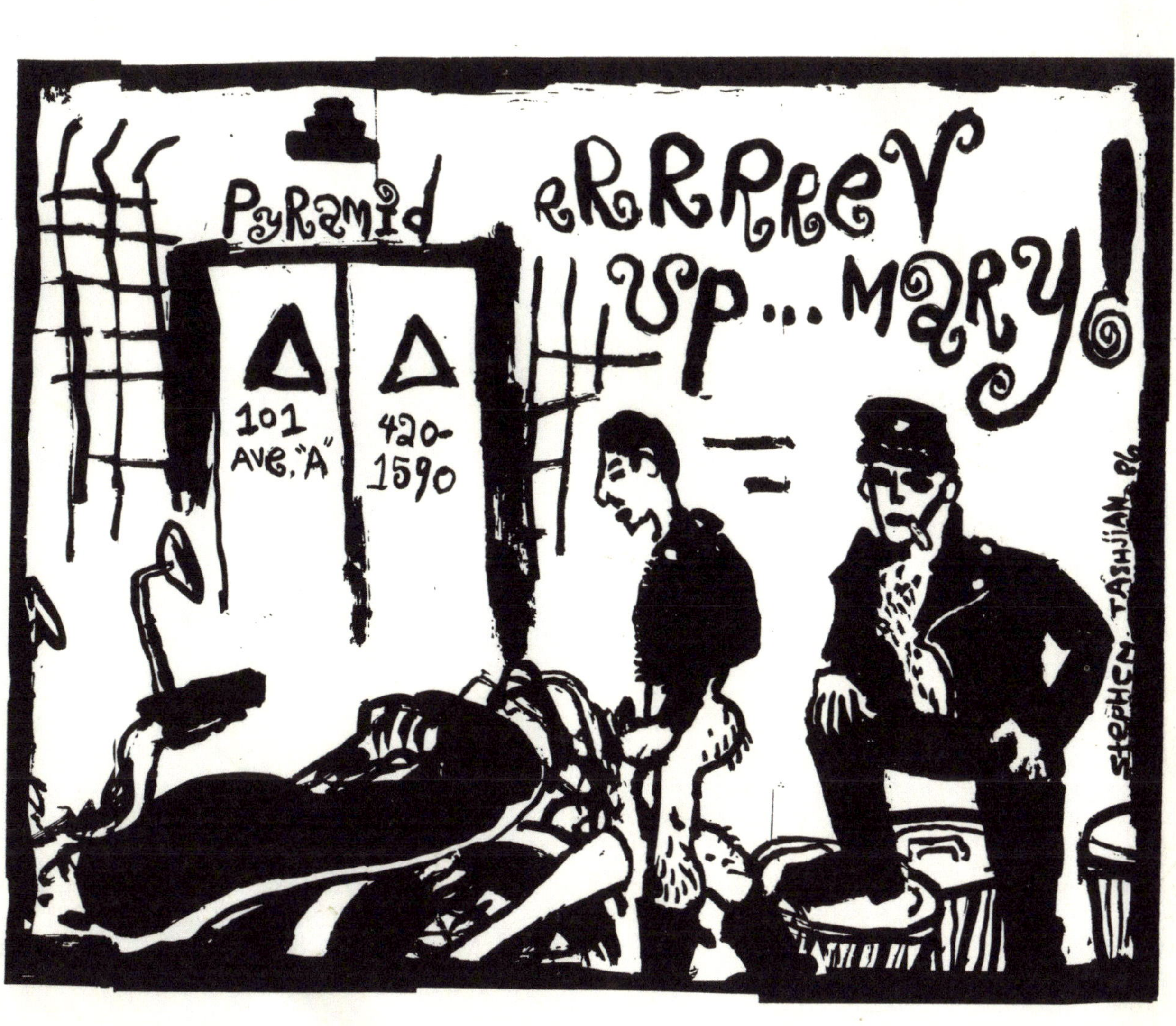

Pyramid Club flyer, 1987, black-and-white photocopy, 8½ × 11 inches (21.6 × 27.9 cm)

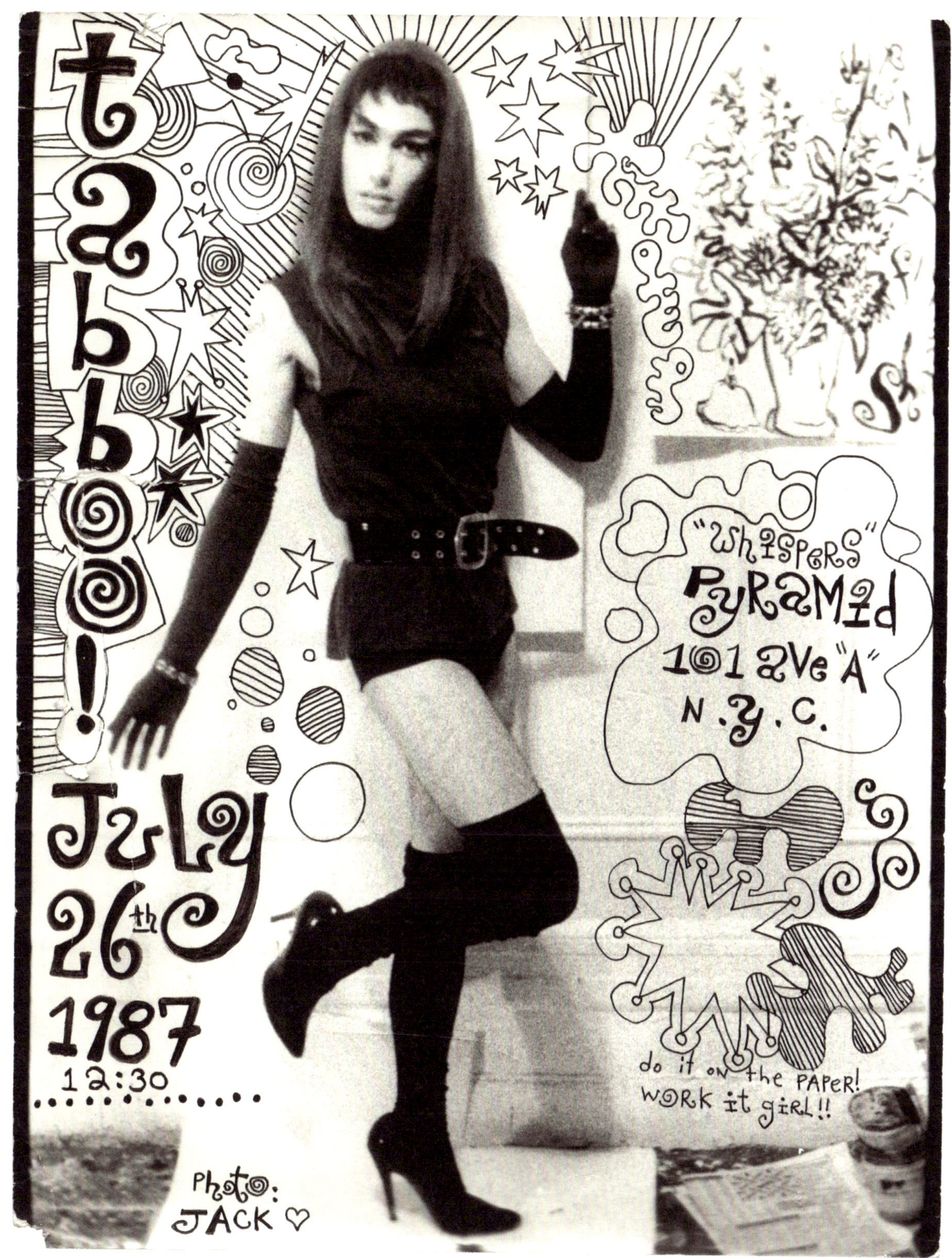

Pyramid Club poster drawing, 1987, pen on gelatin silver print by Jack Pierson, 14 × 11 inches (35.6 × 27.9 cm)

Published on the occasion
of the exhibition

Tabboo! 1982–1988
December 6, 2020–January 10, 2021

Gordon Robichaux
41 Union Square West
#925 and #907
New York, NY 10003

Karma Bookstore
136 E 3rd Street
New York, NY 10009

Published by Karma Books, New York
and Gordon Robichaux, New York

Edition of 1,200
Special edition of 50

Frontispiece:
Clayton Patterson
Tabboo! & David Yarritu, 1986
Color photograph
5 × 3½ inches (12.7 × 8.9 cm)

ISBN 978-1-949172-57-7